ACTION RESEARCH COMMUNITIES

Action Research Communities presents a new perspective on two current and proven educational practices: classroom-/school-based action research and professional learning communities. Implementation of one or the other of these practices often results in a variety of possible benefits for the teaching–learning process, for student achievement, and for overall school improvement. While these might seem to be separate, isolated practices, the author has taken the beneficial aspects of each practice and merged them into a cohesive and potentially powerful concept, coined "action research communities."

Each of the two concepts or approaches (*action research* and *professional learning communities*) is presented and discussed in detail. Because they both focus on local-level improvement of educational practice and share several overlapping features, the two concepts are then merged into a single entity—action research communities, or ARCs. These professional learning communities, with action research at their core, hold an immense amount of power and potential when it comes to enhanced professional growth and development for educators, increased student achievement, school improvement, and educator empowerment. ARCs essentially capitalize on all the individualized benefits and strengths of action research *and* of professional learning communities, and merge them into a single educational concept and practice. ARCs have the potential to help educators everywhere experience:

- a common and collective focus and vision;
- sustained collaborative inquiry;
- individualized, customizable—and meaningful—professional growth; and
- true empowerment that comes with this form of collaborative, inquiry-based, and reflective practice.

Practical guidance for the development and implementation of ARCs is also provided, by focusing on ways in which professional educators (teachers, administrators, support staff, etc.) can implement, sustain, and extend the impact of their respective action research communities. Specific roles for district administrators, building administrators, and teachers are presented and discussed in depth, as are ways that ARCs can be used both to deepen professional learning for educators and to improve student learning.

Craig A. Mertler is an Associate Professor and Director of the EdD Program in Leadership & Innovation at Arizona State University. He has been an educator for 32 years, 22 of those in higher education, and 6 as an administrator. He is the author of 22 books, 8 invited book chapters, and 20 refereed journal articles.

ACTION RESEARCH COMMUNITIES

Professional Learning, Empowerment, and Improvement Through Collaborative Action Research

Craig A. Mertler

LONDON AND NEW YORK

First published 2018
by Routledge
2 Park Square, Milton Park, Abingdon, Oxon OX14 4RN

and by Routledge
711 Third Avenue, New York, NY 10017

Routledge is an imprint of the Taylor & Francis Group, an informa business

© 2018 Craig A. Mertler

The right of Craig A. Mertler to be identified as author of this work has been
asserted by him in accordance with sections 77 and 78 of the Copyright,
Designs and Patents Act 1988.

All rights reserved. No part of this book may be reprinted or
reproduced or utilised in any form or by any electronic, mechanical,
or other means, now known or hereafter invented, including photocopying
and recording, or in any information storage or retrieval system,
without permission in writing from the publishers.

Trademark notice: Product or corporate names may be trademarks
or registered trademarks, and are used only for identification
and explanation without intent to infringe.

British Library Cataloguing-in-Publication Data
A catalogue record for this book is available from the British Library

Library of Congress Cataloging-in-Publication Data
Title: Action research communities : professional learning, empowerment,
and improvement through collaborative action research / Craig A. Mertler.
Description: Abingdon, Oxon ; New York, NY : Routledge, 2017. |
Includes bibliographical references.
Identifiers: LCCN 2017004553| ISBN 9781138057944 (hardback) |
ISBN 9781138057951 (pbk.) | ISBN 9781315164564 (ebook)
Subjects: LCSH: Action research in education. | Professional learning
communities.
Classification: LCC LB1028.24 .M474 2017 | DDC 370.72—dc23
LC record available at https://lccn.loc.gov/2017004553

ISBN: 978-1-138-05794-4 (hbk)
ISBN: 978-1-138-05795-1 (pbk)
ISBN: 978-1-315-16456-4 (ebk)

Typeset in Bembo and Stone Sans
by Florence Production Ltd, Stoodleigh, Devon, UK

CONTENTS

Introduction: Why merge action research and professional learning communities?   **1**

1   What is action research?   **5**

Description of action research   5
Action research vs. educational research   7
What action research is and is not   13
Professional benefits of action research   14
The process of conducting action research   21
The process in action—an example   25

    Step 1: Identifying and limiting the topic   25
    Step 2: Gathering information   26
    Step 3: Reviewing the related literature   26
    Step 4: Developing a research plan   26
    Step 5: Implementing the plan and collecting data   27
    Step 6: Analyzing the data   27
    Step 7: Developing an action plan   28
    Step 8: Sharing and communicating the results   28
    Step 9: Reflecting on the process   28

Important takeaways from Chapter 1   29

2   Professional learning communities   **31**

What is a professional learning community?   31
Characteristics of PLCs   34

vi Contents

Shared mission, vision, values, and goals   35
Collaborative culture with a focus on learning   36
Collective inquiry into best practice and current
reality   36
Action orientation: Learning by doing   37
Commitment to continuous improvement   38
Orientation focused on results   39

The challenge of a changing culture	40
Teaching and assessing in a PLC	45
Important takeaways from Chapter 2	49

3   The action research model for transformational innovation   51

What is the action research model for transformational innovation?	51
The five components of the model	54

Data-driven educational decision-making   55
Data, data, and more data   57
Thinking differently   58
Collaboration   59
Professional reflection   61

One additional (sub)component . . .	62
Implications of the action research model for transformational innovation	64
Important takeaways from Chapter 3	65

4   Putting it all together: Action research communities   67

TI-in-ed + PLC = ARC	67
Specifying the purposes and functioning of an ARC	68
Roles for teachers in ARCs	71
Roles for building administrators in ARCs	74
Roles for district administrators in ARCs	75
Important takeaways from Chapter 4	77

Contents **vii**

5 Where do we go from here? Sustaining and growing your ARC **79**

Ways to sustain ARCs 79

Link reform efforts to existing practices 80
Focus on "why," then on "how" 80
Align actions with words 81
Be flexible, but firm 81
Build a coalition, but don't wait for unanimity 82
Expect mistakes . . . and learn from them 83
Learn by doing, not by additional training 84
Short-term victories . . . and celebrations 85

Ways to extend ARCs 86

Integrating technology 87
Student engagement 88
Grant funding 89
Mini-grants to ARC participants 90
Systems of incentives 91
Components of personnel evaluation systems 95
Action research/innovation conferences 97

Implementation of an ARC represents a process 99
Important takeaways from Chapter 5 100

6 Using ARCs to deepen professional learning and improve student achievement **103**

Action research communities as mechanisms for professional learning 103
Action research communities as mechanisms for improving student achievement 105
Important takeaways from Chapter 6 106

References *109*
Appendix: Action research mentor portfolio templates *113*
Index *125*

INTRODUCTION

Why merge action research and professional learning communities?

Action research and professional learning communities are both educational concepts and practices that have gained a great deal of momentum in our PK–12 schools and districts over the past ten years or so. On the surface, these might seem like isolated concepts—ones that might not see any sort of side-by-side implementation. For some educators, *action research* might be an unknown entity. For those who know a little something about action research, they might see it as an approach to conducting educational research in schools. Additionally, they would tend to consider anything with the word *research* in its name to be something that is formally conducted by people specifically trained in that arena, such as college and university professors or perhaps graduate students. Still, many of these teachers and administrators would not consider action research to be part of their jobs, or even of interest to them.

A similar set of misunderstandings abound when considering the concept of *professional learning communities*. Many educators believe that they are "doing" a professional learning community when they meet every Tuesday morning for an hour to discuss some common topic. Keep in mind that seldom does this conversation stay focused on that particular topic. For those who have a deeper understanding of professional learning communities, there is still a misconception that these learning communities require an excessive amount of time, where the investments far outweigh the benefits. Unfortunately, many of these educators do not believe that professional learning communities should be a part of their jobs.

2 Introduction

There are, however, a great number of educators who have a true understanding of these two educational concepts and practices. For these teachers and administrators who conduct action research or for those who implement professional learning communities—that is, implementing *only* one or the other—there are a plethora of potential benefits for the teaching and learning process, for student achievement, and for overall school improvement. Arguably, it is for this reason that we have begun to see more and more schools and districts put into practice either classroom-based action research or professional learning communities.

So, let's assume—as many of us already know—that action research, as well as professional learning communities, hold various potentials for vast improvements in our schools. However, consider for a moment the potential impact of *merging* the concepts of action research and professional learning communities. If each of these individually possesses such great potential, it would stand to reason that the likely benefits that could result from a merged set of practices might begin to grow exponentially. Please understand, I do not want to mislead you into thinking that this is a situation where we are trying to mix oil and water, or where we are trying to force a square peg into a round hole.

On the contrary, action research and professional learning communities share so many important and key aspects of their foundational structure that finding a way to merge them into a single entity seems to make perfect sense to many educators. This merging into a single entity—a concept that I have coined *action research learning communities*, or more simply, *action research communities*—holds an immense amount of power and potential when it comes to enhanced professional growth and development for educators, increased student achievement, and school improvement. Action research communities, or *ARCs*, essentially capitalize on all of the individualized benefits and strengths of action research and of professional learning communities, and merge them into a single educational concept and practice. ARCs have the potential to help educators everywhere experience:

- a common and collective focus and vision;
- sustained collaborative inquiry;
- individualized, customizable—and meaningful—professional growth; and

Introduction **3**

- true empowerment that comes with this form of collaborative, inquiry-based, and reflective practice.

Therefore, perhaps, the better question for us to bear in mind as we begin to examine the contents of this book might be . . .

Why *not* merge action research and professional learning communities?

1

WHAT IS ACTION RESEARCH?

In Chapter 1 of the book, you will learn more about exactly what action research is and how it relates to the broader field of educational research. While it is fairly similar to the process of conducting educational research, the process of action research has its own unique characteristics. In addition, you will learn about the professional benefits of action research, as well as ways in which action research can be applied in professional educational settings.

Description of action research

"Research" is a term that typically makes many people—especially educators—somewhat uncomfortable. They sometimes equate it with endeavors that they believe to be more "scientific" in nature (e.g., people in white lab coats with beakers and test tubes or perhaps lab animals); or, they may have flashbacks to graduate courses in research methodology and/or statistical analysis. While there may be some degree of accuracy in each of those mental interpretations and connotations, I am a firm believer in the fact that research should be viewed as our ally in the teaching and learning process. The main reason for this belief on my part is the fact that research can provide us with a systematic mechanism for collecting meaningful educational data (e.g., student assessment data, attendance and discipline data, or measures of teacher effectiveness, communication skills, or leadership skills), and then using those data as the basis for well-informed educational decision-making. After all, data-driven—or, perhaps, more appropriately data-*informed*—educational decision-making has become one of the primary focal points—if not *the* focal point—for the work that we collectively do as professional educators. It really does not matter if your professional

6 What is action research?

responsibilities involve working in a position of an early childhood educator, a middle school administrator, or a college or university professor—educational decision-making is no longer reliant upon "gut instinct and reaction"; it now has its basis in hard data, gathered primarily from those whom we are charged to educate, from our colleagues, and from our educational institutions, as a whole.

Any sort of research has its foundation in the application of the scientific method. This is the case, regardless of the field in which the research is being conducted—research in medicine, physics, sociology, astronomy, business, or psychology; the broad field of education is no exception to this fact. We are all undoubtedly familiar with the scientific method; many of us had our formal introduction to it as a process during our middle school years, the first time we conducted and completed a science fair project. We began the process by identifying a topic, then stating a research question that we wanted to answer or a prediction (i.e., a hypothesis) that we wanted to test. We then designed an "experiment" and collected our own empirical data. Once we had analyzed our data, we used the results as evidence necessary to answer our original question or pass judgment on the prediction that we stated at the outset of our study.

While there are numerous similarities between traditional educational research and action research, there is one crucial difference. Action research *is* educational research; however, it is research that is conducted *by* educators *for* themselves (Mertler, 2017). Individuals who are—at least to some degree—removed from the situation and setting that they are investigating often conduct traditional educational research. University professors or graduate research assistants may conduct more traditional forms of research in education, often with an affiliation to a grant-funded project or graduate-level research. In contrast, action research is conducted by the individual or individuals who play an active role and who have a vested interest in the particular setting. Johnson (2012) has described action research as being true systematic inquiry into one's *own* practice. More specifically, Mills (2014) defines action research as any systematic inquiry conducted by teachers, administrators, counselors, or others with a vested interest in the teaching and learning process or environment for the purposes of gathering information about how their particular schools operate, how they teach, and how their students learn.

Action research vs. educational research

As was mentioned above, traditional educational research is routinely conducted by individuals who are somewhat removed from the environment or setting that they are studying. That is not to say that those individuals are not committed to the topics and phenomena that they are studying; they are most certainly interested in the ultimate results related to those studies, and work very diligently to study them as completely as is possible. This simply means that they typically study students and teachers, schools, and educational programs with which they seldom have any specific personal involvement. At this point, let us review some of the basics of traditional research conducted in the broad field of education.

There are essentially three categories of traditional educational research: quantitative research, qualitative research, and mixed-methods research. These three approaches to conducting educational research are distinguished based on the nature of the data that are collected and analyzed. More specifically, these approaches to research are based on different assumptions about how to best understand what is true and accurate about the world or a particular phenomenon of interest, or what comprises the realities or perceptions held by different individuals (McMillan, 2012). Although they should not necessarily be treated as mutually exclusive, let us initially examine each one individually. Generally speaking, *quantitative research* requires the collection and analysis of numerical data (e.g., test scores, ratings of perceptions or opinions, or frequency counts); *qualitative research* methodologies involve the collection and analysis of narrative data (e.g., observation notes, interview transcripts, or journal entries). *Mixed-methods research* includes approaches where both numerical and narrative data are collected and analyzed within the same study.

Quantitative research tends to work from broader ideas and ends with results that are more specific to a particular setting or situation. Researchers begin by stating *research questions* they wish to answer or *hypotheses* they wish to test, then collect data by measuring *variables*— typically a relatively small number of variables. For example, a quantitative research study might require the collection of data on elementary school discipline referrals and absenteeism (numerical variables) in order to answer the following research question: *Are there differences in the rates and types of disciplinary problems and absenteeism in schools*

8 What is action research?

with a K–8 grade span versus those with other grade span configurations (e.g., K–6, 6–8)? (Mertler, 2017). Researchers must also specify a research design—the plan that will be used to carry out the study. Research designs may be described as being either *nonexperimental* or *experimental*. In *nonexperimental* research studies, researchers have no direct control over any variable in the study, either because the variables—or measurements of those variables—have already occurred or because it is not possible or ethical for any of the variables to be controlled or manipulated. Examples of nonexperimental studies include descriptive, comparative, correlational, and causal-comparative research. *Descriptive* studies simply report information about the frequency or amount of something that has occurred. *Comparative* studies build on descriptive studies by not only reporting the frequency of something, but then also comparing two or more groups on the variable(s) that have been measured. *Correlational* studies measure the degree to which two or more variables are related. Finally, *causal-comparative* studies (also sometimes referred to as *ex post facto* studies) compare groups—where group membership has been determined by something that occurred in the past (e.g., gender or class membership)—on subsequent data collected on another variable.

In *experimental* research studies, the researcher actually has some degree of control over one or more of the variables included in the study; this variable may serve as an influence or cause of participants' behavior. The variable over which the researcher has control is known as the *independent variable*. Independent variables are those that are manipulated by the researcher—meaning that the researcher determines which participants in the study will receive which (of two or more) conditions. In the simplest experimental designs, there are two groups: the *treatment* group and the *comparison* group. For example, the treatment group would receive a condition that is seen as being new, innovative, or simply different; whereas, the comparison group would receive the condition that has typically been utilized in the past. The ultimate variable of interest—the behavior or performance, for example—is referred to as the *dependent variable* and is measured for both groups. The scores on the dependent variable (for each of the two or more conditions or groups) are then compared.

Data collected during quantitative research studies are numerical and are, therefore, analyzed statistically. The analyses of quantitative data may include descriptive statistics, inferential statistics, or both. *Descriptive statistics* allow researchers to summarize, organize, and simplify large amounts of data. Specific techniques include the calculation of such statistics as the mean, median, mode, range, standard deviation, correlations, and standardized scores. The use of *inferential statistics* involves more complex mathematical procedures, and enables researchers to test the statistical significance of the difference between two groups or the degree of relationship between two or more variables. Commonly used inferential statistical techniques include *t*-tests, analysis of variance (ANOVA), and regression. As mentioned, inferential statistics enable the researcher to test the size of the difference between groups or strength of the relationship between variables for statistical significance. *Statistical significance* refers to the extent to which the results of the statistical analysis (e.g., the treatment group scored higher than the comparison group) will enable researchers to conclude that the findings of a given study are large enough in the *sample* studied in order to represent a meaningful difference or relationship in the *population* from which the sample was selected.

Qualitative research begins with observations that are much more specific, with the goal of making much broader conclusions at the end of the study. The focus of qualitative research is typically broader and much more holistic, focusing on a large number of potential variables. There is no attempt to control variables in a qualitative research study; researchers study the "world" as it exists. The research questions that guide qualitative research studies tend to be more broad and open-ended when compared to their quantitative counterparts. This, therefore, encourages the use of multiple types of measures and observations, such as observations with recorded notes, interviews with recorded transcripts, and journals—all of which results in the collection of narrative data. This collection of a wide variety of data for the purposes of getting a more holistic picture of the topic or phenomenon which serves as the focus of the study also permits the researcher to engage in a process known as triangulation. *Triangulation* is a process of relating multiple sources and types of data in order to verify the accuracy and consistency of the observations made in a qualitative research study. Often, people will interpret "triangulation" as meaning that there must be three (as in *tri-*)—no more, no less—sources of data. This is not entirely accurate, as the specific number of sources or types of data is

10 What is action research?

dictated by the research situation at hand. It is for this reason that I sometimes prefer the use of the term "*polyangulation*" (since the prefix *poly-* is defined as "more than one or many") (Mertler, 2017).

Similar to quantitative research, there are a variety of designs that can be used in a qualitative research study. These designs include phenomenology, ethnography, grounded theory, and case studies, among others. *Phenomenological studies* require that the researchers engage in a lengthy process of individual interviews in an attempt to fully and completely understand a particular research topic. *Ethnographic studies* attempt to describe social interactions between people in intact group settings. *Grounded theory research studies* try to discover a theory that somehow relates to a particular environment, situation, or setting. Finally, *case studies* are in-depth investigations of individual and specific programs, activities, people, or groups. Although all data will be narrative in form, the data collected during a qualitative research study may be quite diverse. These data are then analyzed by means of a process known as *logico-inductive analysis*, which is a thought process that makes use of logic in order to uncover patterns and trends across all the various types of data collected.

It is probably very obvious to you that quantitative and qualitative approaches to conducting educational research are quite different on a variety of levels. Decades ago, researchers in education treated the two approaches to research as if they were entirely independent of one another. Realistically, however, it makes some degree of sense that educational research studies could and should employ both types of designs and data. These types of studies are referred to as *mixed-methods research studies*. The distinct benefit of mixed-methods studies is that the combination of both types of data tends to provide a better and more thorough understanding of the research problem, as opposed to simply using one type of data in isolation. In other words, these types of studies essentially capitalize on the strengths of *both* quantitative and qualitative data. Mixed-methods research studies have become widely accepted as an approach to investigating educational problems.

So, how does action research relate to educational research? Simply put—and to reiterate an earlier point—action research *is* educational research. Action research studies can use any of the designs—quantitative, qualitative, or mixed-methods—that have been discussed above. In fact, Creswell (2005) considers mixed-methods designs and action research studies to be very similar to one another, since they both often utilize quantitative and qualitative data, but that does not mean that action research studies cannot rely purely on either quantitative or qualitative approaches. The only real difference between action research and any of the approaches to conducting more traditional forms of educational research has little—if anything—to do with a specific approach, research design, or type of data, but rather rests solely in the *underlying purpose for the research*. The main goal of quantitative research is to describe and explain a research problem; that for qualitative research is to develop a holistic description of a research situation, often for the purposes of developing theory. The purpose of mixed-methods studies is similar to traditional quantitative research (i.e., to better understand and explain a research problem). However, *the main goal of action research is to address local-level problems of practice with the anticipation of finding immediate answers to questions or solutions to those problems.*

At this point, a note about problems of practice may be warranted. There is a tendency for educators to mistakenly equate educational *problems* with *problems of practice*. Generally speaking, problems are extremely abundant in educational settings. However, problems— in and of themselves—are not directly "solvable." For example, in speaking with a classroom teacher, you might become aware of the following problem in a classroom or school: *my students do not perform well in math*. By definition, this is not a problem of practice. Henriksen and Richardson (2016) have described a "problem of practice" as follows:

> There is no single standard definition for "problem of practice" in education. But it is often understood as a problem or issue of a complex and significant, yet still actionable and context-driven, nature. It represents an issue that exists within a professional's sphere of work (City, Elmore, Fiarman, & Teitel, 2009). The term is not typically used to constitute problems that are minor or easily solvable. It speaks to issues that are impactful in a prac-titioner's work and context. Problems of practice are observable (either directly or indirectly), and often involve multiple stake-holders and variables. Such issues are personal in that, while they may connect with broader or common issues of the profession,

12 What is action research?

they are also uniquely tied to a context and its variables. Thus, such issues can be navigated by knowledgeable practitioners in the context they emerge within (Lampert, 1985). These characteristics give them a sense of personal impact and scale within their local context. Therefore, the range of possible educational problems of practice that could exist is as unlimited as the variables and contexts that exist in teaching, learning, research, and other educational practice.

A simple transition to a problem of practice from the problem of students not performing well in math might be:

The students in my class do not perform well in math. What might I be able to do differently with my instruction that could facilitate improvement in my students' math skills and performance?

In other words, a problem of practice must be situated within a professional educator's scope of work and must be specific to the particular setting, students, and context. This is essentially what distinguishes a *problem*, which could potentially occur anywhere in the world—such as students not performing well in math—from a problem of practice, which consists of the problem, situated within a particular context, and includes specific strategies for solving the problem, or otherwise addressing the issue, where the concern is essentially localized.

It is important to note that it was not my intent in this section—nor is it the purpose of this book in its entirety—to familiarize the reader with the details of conducting traditional educational research. If the reader is interested in more detailed discussions of the various specifics, requirements, and applications of traditional educational research, including data collection and analyses, the reader is advised to refer to any of the following: *Introduction to Educational Research*, 1st edition (Mertler, 2016); *Educational Research: Planning, Conducting, and Evaluating Quantitative and Qualitative Research*, 2nd edition (Creswell, 2005); *Designing and Conducting Mixed Methods Research*, 2nd edition (Creswell & Plano Clark, 2011); *Educational Research: Competencies for Analysis and Applications*, 9th edition (Gay, Mills, & Airasian, 2009);

and *Educational Research: Fundamentals for the Consumer*, 6th edition (McMillan, 2012).

What action research *is* and *is not*

There are many aspects of the process of engaging in the action research process that characterize its uniqueness as an approach to conducting educational research. I believe that it is critical for educators—at all levels and professional positions—to have a sound, foundational understanding of exactly what action research is and is not. The following list is an attempt to describe what action research *is* (Mertler, 2017, pp. 19–21). Action research is . . .

- A process that improves education, in general, by incorporating change.
- A process involving educators working together to improve their own practices.
- Persuasive and authoritative, since it is done by teachers for teachers.
- Collaborative; that is, it is composed of educators talking and working with other educators in empowering relationships.
- Participative, since educators are integral members—not disinterested outsiders—of the research process.
- Practical and relevant to classroom teachers, since it allows them direct access to research findings.
- Developing critical reflection about one's teaching.
- A planned, systematic approach to understanding the learning process.
- A process that requires us to "test" our ideas about education.
- Open-minded.
- A critical analysis of educational places of work.
- A cyclical process of planning, acting, developing, and reflecting.
- A justification of one's teaching practices.

In order to truly understand what action research *is*, educators must also understand what it *is not* (Mertler, 2017, p. 21). Action research is not . . .

14 What is action research?

- The usual thing that teachers do when thinking about teaching; it is more systematic and more collaborative.
- Simply problem solving; it involves the specification of a problem, the development of something new (in most cases), and critical reflection on its effectiveness.
- Done "to" or "by" other people; it is research done by particular educators, on their own work, with students and colleagues.
- The simple implementation of predetermined answers to educational questions; it explores, discovers, and works to find creative solutions to educational problems.
- Conclusive; the results of action research are neither right nor wrong but rather tentative solutions that are based on observations and other data collection and that require monitoring and evaluation in order to identify strengths and limitations.
- A fad; good teaching has always involved the systematic examination of the instructional process and its effects on student learning. Teachers are always looking for ways to improve instructional practice, and although teachers seldom have referred to this process of observation, revision, and reflection as research, that is precisely what it is.

Professional benefits of action research

When I talk with educators about the virtues of routine and regular engagement in the action research process, that presentation is sometimes met with a degree of skepticism. During workshops or other types of professional development that I have led, educators have typically asked alternative forms of three basic questions. First, they often have a difficult time trying to discern exactly where in their days, months, and school year they will be able to find time to "do" action research. I have actually been asked—on several occasions—the following question: "*Why should I become involved in an action research project, especially with all the demands and responsibilities placed on me as an educator?*" Although this question is a very realistic and legitimate one, it is a question to which I do not have difficulty responding:

> First, action research deals with your problems, not someone else's. Second, action research is very timely; it can start now—

What is action research? **15**

or whenever you are ready—and [can] provide immediate results. Third, action research provides educators with opportunities to better understand, and therefore improve, their educational practices. Fourth, as a process, action research can also promote the building of stronger relationships among colleagues with whom we work. Finally, and possibly most importantly, action research provides educators with alternative ways of viewing and approaching educational questions and problems and with new ways of examining our own educational practices.

(Mertler, 2017, p. 21)

A second question that is often posed—usually as a follow-up to the first one—is some variation of the following: "*If the benefits of action research are so substantial, why isn't everyone doing it?*" Hmm . . . good question. I tend to offer the following as a response:

First, although its popularity has increased over the past decade, action research is still relatively unknown when compared to more traditional forms of conducting research. Second, although it may not seem the case, action research [may be] more difficult to conduct than traditional approaches to research. Educators themselves are responsible for implementing the resultant changes, but also for conducting the research. Third, action research does not conform to many of the requirements of conventional research with which you may be familiar—it is therefore less structured and more difficult to conduct. Finally, because of the lack of fit between standard research requirements and the process of conducting action research, you may find it more difficult to write up your results.

(Mertler, 2017, p. 22)

Although I have not been asked the third and final question nearly as often, invariably there will be someone in an audience of professional educators who asks: "*Why should I do all of this extra work, if I'm not being paid to do it?*" Now, please understand that by the time that this question comes up during the presentation, I have established a good degree of rapport with my audience of educators, so my innate sarcasm tends to surface (just a bit). My response is pithy, but to the point:

16 What is action research?

> Well, I'm not sure. [pause, for effect . . .] Why would you want to become a better teacher, especially if you're not being paid to become a better teacher? [another pause for effect . . .]
>
> (Mertler, 2009a, p. 23)

Please do not mistake my sarcasm for a lack of understanding or compassion. I have been a professional educator for more than three decades—including several years as a high school science teacher; I fully understand where these people are coming from. However, my argument is that if educators engage in action research as part of their daily work routine—which does not mean that it has to be done every day, but rather that it becomes part of a professional routine—then, it also becomes part of annual professional development. Granted, it requires a different mindset—a different approach—to the work of being a professional educator. However, if we can collectively embrace action research as an integral part of our work, it honestly just becomes part of the job of being a quality educator.

Let us briefly consider Finland, as an example. As we all know, Finland has been held up in recent years as an exemplary national system of education. I have had numerous conversations with people who have studied the Finnish system of education. When it comes to the topic of action research, there appears to be a great deal of agreement. Consider the following comments, written by Karen Lee (Lee, 2013), a social studies teacher from Washington, D.C., who recently traveled to and studied the Finnish education system as part of the Distinguished Fulbright Award in Teaching program. While working in Jyväskylä, Finland, for seven months, Ms. Lee engaged in an action research project of her own. Here is what she had to say about Finnish teachers and their teacher training programs:

> Teacher training programs in Finland focus on providing teachers the tools to be researchers, to look at their lessons and classes and critically analyze the teaching process and how to improve. They are taught to be reflective thinkers and deliver research-based strategies in lessons. Teachers are asked to continually integrate theory and practice while receiving feedback and support from their peers. A "teacher's duty is to transform the knowledge he or she knows into a form the learner can adopt"

(Helsinki Teacher Training Handbook). In order to do that, teachers have to be researchers. They have to continually push themselves to think about the *why* and *how* behind a lesson [emphasis added]. . . . When trying to understand the global success of Finnish education, it is important to start with understanding the uniform teaching training process and the expectation that teachers continue to be an example of a life-long learner and grow in their profession.

(Lee, 2013)

In a nutshell, Finnish teachers are trained to be reflective in all that they do; this is a central tenet of action research. Further, one of the main focal points for the practicing Finnish educator is continual growth and professional development. Action research is one highly effective mechanism for achieving these types of professional goals.

So, my final comment to educators who question the ultimate value of integrating an action research mindset and approach to their work is as follows:

> "With the potential benefits in engaging in a process like this, how can you afford *not* to try it? Can you honestly afford *not* to see how it might work for you?"

In my opinion, there are five broad categories or ways in which action research can be successfully integrated into educational settings (Mertler, 2017). These are listed and briefly discussed below. Action research can be used to . . .

1. *Connect theory to practice*—Research is often used as a mechanism for developing theories that are designed to eventually help determine best practices in educational settings. These best practices, in turn, are then used by educators to develop effective and meaningful learning experiences for their students. However, we often discover a "gap" that exists between the findings of research studies—as conducted by researchers, university professors, and graduate students—and the applicability of those findings—that are to be implemented by practicing educators—in today's classrooms. Often, these research results are not disseminated in a way that makes them useful to the practicing educator. Many educators believe that traditional educational research is simply impractical and irrelevant to their needs.

18 What is action research?

Action research can provide one possible solution to bridging this gap by encouraging a two-way flow of information. In addition to information that flows from the researcher to the practitioner as a result of traditional research, data collected and analyzed by practicing educators in their own classrooms can be used to inform research *directly* related to best practices. This is possible since the classroom research—i.e., *action research*—is being conducted firsthand by the practitioner.

2. *Improve educational practice*—A main focus of action research is the improvement of classroom practice, through professional reflection and critical examination of one's own praxis. Through this focus on reflection, as well as collaboration, action research can ultimately lead to improvements in the way educators do their jobs, the successes they experience, and the meaningful learning experiences they provide for their students.

As I mentioned earlier, this does require a shift in mindset, a shift in the way we think about and approach our own professional practice. Gone are the days when teachers believed that they had mastered their profession simply as a result of spending years in the classroom. Further, "success" cannot be defined as simply continuing to do what has been done for years. True experts or "master teachers" are those who constantly and systematically reflect on their actions and performance, as well as the consequences of those actions. This continuing reflection results in the acquisition of new information and knowledge that helps to guide successful efforts in the future. Systematic reflection as part of an action research process is capable of providing this stimulus for change and the improvement of educational practice.

3. *Foster broad school improvement*—Up to this point, we have really discussed action research as it pertains to improving *individual* classroom practice. However, action research can also be facilitated so that it promotes more widespread types of improvements, as well. One way to accomplish broader school improvement—for example, grade-level, school-level, or district-level improvements—is through the use of action research as a collaborative venture. Collaboratively designed and implemented action research—a concept known as *collaborative action research* (or *CAR*)—is ideal for engaging teachers, administrators, and support personnel in systemic, self-initiated school improvement.

4. *Empower educators and engage them intellectually*—I have saved what I believe to be the two most important uses or applications of action

What is action research? **19**

research for the end of this list. I believe that action research is very effective at advancing the notion of *educator empowerment*. With each passing year, the educational climate in this country becomes more and more data-driven in its approach to education and educational decision-making. When teachers collect data, analyze those data, and systematically reflect on their own teaching and their students' learning—followed by the use of all of that information to help them make better informed educational decisions—they truly become empowered. This empowerment allows them to utilize their own unique sets of expertise, talents, and creativity so that they can implement instructional programs that will best meet the needs of their students. The educators themselves become the appropriate judges to determine when and where risk-taking and instructional change may be appropriate and beneficial.

When educators engage in this kind of work, they begin to assume different roles within their schools—for example, the roles of facilitator, supporter, and mentor. While the skills and abilities of building- and district-level administrators will always be necessary and needed, the "locus of control" is essentially returned to the classroom level when teachers begin to assume these different roles. When a greater level of "control" is returned to the classroom teacher, the effectiveness of schools is enhanced and school improvement is promoted (Johnson, 2012).

An additional benefit that accompanies an increased level of empowerment is a greater level of *intellectual engagement* with respect to all that goes on within their classrooms, as well as within the school as a whole. The experiences and skills that teachers gain through engagement in a process of reflective action research are beneficial not only within the parameters of that which they are critically examining, but are also transferable to other professional activities, including those daily activities associated with running an effective and efficient classroom.

5. *Cultivate professional growth*—Finally, and perhaps most importantly, I firmly believe that there is an incredibly strong connection between the implementation of action research and the professional growth and development of educators. Action research permits an educator the opportunity to focus his or her professional growth on specific things that that individual—or, perhaps, a collaborative group

20 What is action research?

of educators—identifies as being an area of professional practice that they would like to improve (Mertler, 2013b). Gone are—or, at least should be—the days of "one-size-fits-all" forms of professional development, since this form of professional development does not target the *specific* needs of *individual* educators. In the early 1980s, action research began being promoted as a meaningful alternative to more "typical" in-service training and professional development for educators. Oliver (1980) argued that the major benefit of action research as in-service training is that it promotes a continuing process of professional development in a climate where teachers, administrators, and other school personnel not only pose the research questions, but also test their own solutions, as well. Additionally, once educators have the results from their own action research studies, they have the ability to take action immediately. This, in and of itself, results in professional development that would certainly be more meaningful for educators (Mertler, 2013b).

More "enlightened" forms of professional learning and development (McNiff, 2002) operate under the assumption that a vast majority of professional educators already possess a good deal of professional knowledge, and are highly capable of furthering their *own* [emphasis added] learning. These types of professional learning opportunities capitalize on a more appropriate form of support to help educators celebrate what they already know, but also encourage them to develop their own new knowledge. An action research approach lends itself very nicely to this process, in that it requires educators to evaluate what they are doing and further to assess how effectively they are doing so (Mertler & Hartley, 2017).

One-size-fits-all-type professional development programs or activities simply do not accomplish this. Additionally, once an educator has results from the implementation of action research, he or she has the ability to take action immediately. This, in and of itself, will undoubtedly result in professional development that is much more meaningful for individual educators everywhere (Mertler, 2013b). If we collectively rely on the dissemination of "proven" research-based solutions, we typically must wait—sometimes for several years—for the accumulation of evidence that demonstrates relative effectiveness. Furthermore, this proven solution may be subject to weaknesses related to the potential limited generalizability and transferability of the evidence. When educators systematically investigate their own instruction, practices, classrooms, and students, they collect data and other information on their *own* teaching; they know immediately what works and what may not work.

Action research—the act of systematically and reflectively investigating one's own professional practice for the overarching goal of improving that practice—is the *epitome* of customizable and meaningful professional development for educators. As a process, action research allows districts and individual schools to focus on meeting the challenges that are contextually unique to their individual settings. This could possibly be the single most effective strategy for identifying local-level problems of practice, implementing innovative solutions, and initiating positive change in our schools. "There is no single, pre-packaged, commercially-available 'solution' to widespread educational problems of practice that can accomplish what the application of the action research process can do" (Mertler & Hartley, 2017).

The process of conducting action research

I view action research as a four-stage cyclical process. This process consists of the following stages or phases:

1. The *planning* stage—planning for your action research
2. The *acting* stage—taking action on the plan
3. The *developing* stage—developing an action plan for implementation and future cycles of action research
4. The *reflecting* stage—reflecting on the process

This four-stage cyclical process is depicted in Figure 1.1.

While this figure allows the reader to see the overall cyclical nature of action research, it is critical to examine the specific activities that occur in each of the four stages. There are nine specific research activities that fall within these four stages. These nine steps—as they are embedded within the four stages—are as follows:
The Planning Stage:

1. Identifying and limiting a topic
2. Gathering related information

22 What is action research?

3. Reviewing related literature
4. Developing a research plan

The Acting Stage:

5. Collecting data
6. Analyzing data

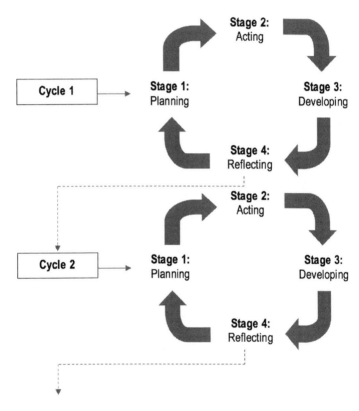

Cyclical process of action research continues...

FIGURE 1.1 The cyclical process of action research
(Mertler, 2017)

The Developing Stage:

7. Developing an action plan

The Reflecting Stage:

8. Sharing and communicating the results
9. Reflecting on the process

An expanded visual depiction of the action research process appears in Figure 1.2. For a much more detailed presentation on the four stages and nine steps involved in conducting action research, the reader is advised to refer to *Action Research: Improving Schools and Empowering Educators*, 5th edition (Mertler, 2017).

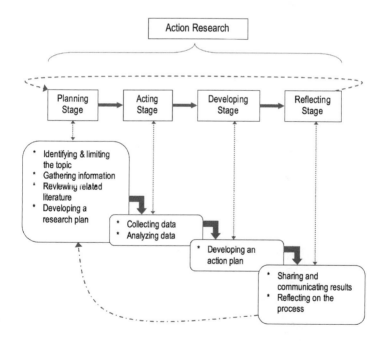

FIGURE 1.2 The cyclical process of action research, showing the four stages and the nine research activities

(Mertler, 2017)

24 What is action research?

It is critical to point out two important features of the procedural diagrams, as shown in Figures 1.1 and 1.2. First, the diagrams may appear somewhat linear—or, at least, to include linear components—although, this is merely to show the relationships that exist between adjacent stages or steps. The process of action research is actually cyclical in nature. Whereas action research has a clear beginning, it does not have a clearly defined endpoint. Typically, educators design and implement an action research project (e.g., perhaps an intervention strategy, or a new instructional method), collect and analyze data in order to evaluate its effectiveness, and then make revisions and improvements for future implementation. In all likelihood, the educator would implement the project again—perhaps with next semester's or next year's students—when the effectiveness would again be monitored and subsequent revisions made. A given project may never have a clear ending, and; there may be subsequent cycles of implementation, evaluation, and revision from one semester or one year to the next. In contrast, however, a professional educator could achieve a level of satisfaction with the effectiveness of an intervention strategy or new instructional method. In this case, the educator would then begin to routinely implement the improved, more effective strategy.

Second, this cyclical nature of action research is actually facilitated by something discussed in the previous paragraph. Notice that dashed arrows connect the reflecting stage to the planning stage of the subsequent cycle. This is due to the fact that the outcome, results, and/or reflections from one cycle provide the impetus for the next cycle of action research. This is a critical feature of action research, in that action research never really ends or stops, the same way that an educator's professional growth never stops. The action research may continue along the same line (i.e., topic or problem of interest) in subsequent cycles, or it may branch off in a different direction. This is not unlike an educator's professional growth and development; sometimes, we feel the need to further our professional development in a single particular area, whereas other times, we feel that we need to branch off and grow in a different direction.

It is important to note, as we are reminded by Johnson (2012), that the nine steps of the action research process are meant to serve as *guidelines* when actually conducting an action research study. They

What is action research? **25**

should be adapted to particular research problems or topics, as needed. Furthermore, it may be appropriate that some steps are skipped altogether, rearranged in terms of their order, or repeated in some instances, depending on the need dictated by the particular action research study. The key to worthwhile practitioner-conducted action research rests in the questions or problems that are addressed by the project and the extent to which the ultimate results are meaningful and important to *that* educator (Parsons & Brown, 2002), and not necessarily in the means by which those results were obtained.

The process in action—an example

As a brief example of the nine-step process in conducting action research, consider the following example (Mertler, 2017, pp. 44–47). The example involves the department chair of a high school social studies department who, for some time, has been disappointed in the performance of students in the school's American history course. The course has always been taught in a traditional manner—with the content coverage beginning prior to the American Revolution and ending with events more recent. The department chair, who teaches multiple sections of the course along with another teacher, believes that there may be some merit in examining a "backward" approach to teaching history (i.e., beginning with current events and proceeding back through time in order to end at the American Revolution). The chair asks the other history teacher for assistance with this potential action research project, and she agrees.

Step 1: Identifying and limiting the topic

The two teachers meet on a couple of occasions over the summer in order to identify the specific topic they hope to address through the examination and trial of this alternative instructional approach. They determine that they believe that their students struggle most in making connections between seemingly unrelated historical events. The department chair argues that perhaps this backward approach (i.e., beginning with more recent historical events with which their students will be more familiar) will have a positive impact on how well they are able to make these types of connections. The teachers decide to focus their

26 What is action research?

attention on any differences that the two instructional approaches have on students' abilities to make these connections.

Step 2: Gathering information

The teachers decide to talk with the other social studies teachers, as well as teachers in other subject areas, in their building. They want to know what other teachers think about their assumption that students struggle with making connections between historical events, which occurred perhaps decades apart. They ask the others for their initial perceptions about the backward approach to teaching their content. Additionally, the two teachers spend time, independently, over the course of a few days to actually consider *why* they believe this is the case for the struggles their students seem to experience. In other words, they carefully consider any "evidence" that may have led them to feel this way. They also strongly consider other possible solutions to this dilemma. At their next meeting together, they share what they had reflected on and decide that the backward approach continues to be worthy of investigating.

Step 3: Reviewing the related literature

The teachers then decide to collect more formal information—that based on research, in addition to what they had already obtained anecdotally from other teachers of history—about the effectiveness of backward approaches to teaching historical, chronological events; how other history teachers may have implemented this type of instruction; and any problems they may have encountered. They decide to split the tasks, with the department chair identifying and reviewing published research studies on the topic and the other teacher contacting history teachers through their professional organizations.

Step 4: Developing a research plan

Following the review of published literature and discussions with teachers from other schools and districts that have implemented this type of instruction, the teachers found enough evidence to support the focus of their proposed study (i.e., the backward approach to instruction is effective), although they also found some contradictory evidence (i.e., this approach is less or at least no more effective). The teachers decide on the following researchable question: *Is there a difference in instructional effectiveness between a backward approach and a forward approach to teaching American history?* Furthermore, based on their review of related literature and other information, the teachers state the following predicted hypothesis: *Students who are exposed to the backward approach will experience higher academic achievement, as evidenced by their abilities to make connections between historical events, than those exposed to the more traditional forward approach.*

Since their hypothesis implies a comparison study, the teachers decide to randomly split the eight sections of American history for the coming school year. Each teacher will teach four sections of American history— for each teacher, two sections will be taught using the forward approach and two sections will incorporate the backward approach. Achievement data, as well as other teacher-developed assessment data, will be collected from all students enrolled in the American history course for this academic year.

Step 5: Implementing the plan and collecting data

Throughout the school year, the two history teachers design perform-ance-based assessments, which examine the extent to which students were able to connect historical events. In addition, students will take an American history achievement test in the spring, a portion of which focuses on critical thinking skills as they apply to historical events.

Step 6: Analyzing the data

Immediately following the end of the school year, data analysis is undertaken. Test scores resulting from the administration of the standardized achievement tests are statistically compared for the two groups (i.e., the backward group versus the forward group). It is determined that the test scores of the students who were taught using the backward instructional approach are significantly higher than those of the students taught in the more traditional manner. In other words, the original research hypothesis has been supported.

28 What is action research?

In addition, scores resulting from the various administrations of classroom-based performance assessments support the results of the standardized achievement tests. Again, the research hypothesis has been supported.

Step 7: Developing an action plan

With their findings in hand, the teachers decide to approach their principal and district curriculum coordinator about temporarily revising the American history curriculum in order to capitalize on the apparent effectiveness of the backward instructional approach. They agree that it will be imperative to continue to implement this strategy and to study the effectiveness of the approach in subsequent academic years. Similar findings in the coming years would provide a much stronger case for permanently changing the approach to teaching American history.

Step 8: Sharing and communicating the results

The principal and curriculum coordinator are quite impressed with the results of this action research study. They suggest to the department chair that the two teachers make a presentation to the school board and to the entire school faculty at a regularly scheduled meeting at the beginning of the next school year. The two teachers develop and make an effective presentation at the subsequent month's board meeting. A teacher attending the board meeting later suggests that this study might make an interesting contribution at an annual state-wide conference on instructional innovations and best practices held each fall.

Step 9: Reflecting on the process

Over the summer, the two teachers meet in order to debrief and decide on any adjustments to the process that might be beneficial for the following year. They consider several questions, including:

- How well did the process work?
- Are we sure that the data we collected were the most appropriate in order to answer our research question?

What is action research? **29**

- Were there additional types of data that could or should have been included in the data collection?

Their answers to these questions will help guide next year's implementation of the backward approach to teaching American history.

Important takeaways from Chapter 1

- Educational research has its basic foundation in the application of the scientific method to educational phenomena.
- Traditional research in education is typically conducted by individuals somewhat removed from the setting they are studying; action research is conducted by individuals with a vested interest in the topic, problem, or setting.
- Three categories of research methods include quantitative approaches, qualitative approaches, and mixed-methods research.
- Quantitative research relies on data that are numerical or that can be quantified.
- Qualitative research utilizes data that are narrative.
- Mixed-methods research makes use of both numerical and narrative data.
- Action research is a form of educational research; the only real difference is its underlying purpose.
- The main goal of action research is to address local-level problems with the anticipation of finding immediate answers to questions or solutions to problems.
- Numerous characteristics distinguish action research from other forms of educational research; it is critical to understand what action research is and is not.
- Professional benefits of action research include: (1) connecting theory to practice, (2) improving educational practice, (3) fostering broad school improvement, (4) empowering educators and engaging them intellectually, and (5) cultivating professional growth.
- Action research is the epitome of customizable and meaningful professional development for educators.

30 What is action research?

- The process of conducting action research consists of four stages (i.e., the planning, acting, developing, and reflecting stages) and nine specific steps or activities.
- Action research is a cyclical process, which has a clear beginning but may not have a specific endpoint.

2

PROFESSIONAL LEARNING COMMUNITIES

In Chapter 2, you will learn more about professional learning communities—what they are, how they are intended to function, their fundamental characteristics, and how they can facilitate a change in the culture of a school or district. This information will help you as you proceed throughout the remainder of the book, as we begin to "connect" action research and professional learning communities.

What is a professional learning community?

Over the past couple of decades, the concept of "school reform" has been an evolving entity. The focus at the level of individual states on standards, minimum competency, outcomes-based education, and accountability really became the driving force in school reform and improvement in the United States during this period of time. With the advent of large-scale federal initiatives such as the No Child Left Behind (NCLB) Act in 2001, Race To The Top (RTTT) in 2009, and the Common Core State Standards (CCSS) in 2010, these types of improvement efforts, which before had been essentially left up to each state to develop and implement, were now being broadened, in order to assume a national "identity" of enhanced accountability and—hopefully—improvement of our nation's education system. My point in raising this brief discussion of these efforts is most certainly *not* to argue for or against their effectiveness, but rather to argue in favor of the fact that professional learning communities offer an incredibly viable alternative mechanism for pursuing local-level school improvement to those efforts that have received national (and international) attention.

Arguably, the utmost authorities on the concept of professional learning communities in schools are DuFour, DuFour, and Eaker

32 Professional learning communities

(2008). They have collectively argued—and made a very convincing case—for the valuable work that can result when the various members of schools and districts collectively commit to functioning as a professional learning community. They have defined a *professional learning community* (or *PLC*) as follows:

> We define a professional learning community as educators committed to working collaboratively in ongoing processes of collective inquiry and action research to achieve better results for the students they serve. Professional learning communities operate under the assumption that the key to improved learning for students is continuous, job-embedded learning for educators.
>
> (DuFour, DuFour, & Eaker, 2008, p. 14)

I have to be honest—I *love* this definition, primarily because it contains so many important aspects that serve as fundamental characterizations of PLCs, many of which we will look at in detail momentarily, but also because they have become focal points for me in my work. Before we look at them in detail, let me highlight several of those aspects here. First, PLCs require a *commitment* on the part of educators. Second, there is a focus on *professional collaboration*, not only in general, but also as it relates to *ongoing collective inquiry and action research*. Third, notice that the ultimate focus of the work of a PLC is on the *achievement of better results for the students* served by these educators. Finally, a key to improved student learning is *job-embedded professional learning for educators*.

It is probably this last point that truly gives me pause to think, as a professional educator. For many, many, many years, professional development in education was approached using a "one-size-fits-all" model. You briefly read a little about my strong feelings concerning this fact in Chapter 1. When I began my career in education nearly thirty years ago, it was not atypical for *all* of the teachers in a school— or perhaps they were separated by grade level or content area, etc.— to attend the same professional development trainings throughout the school year. Perhaps, all the elementary teachers would attend a workshop on early literacy skills. Or, maybe, all of the science teachers would attend a training on the incorporation of inquiry-based learning into their science classes. Here is the difficulty that I have with this model:

Professional learning communities **33**

what if I am an elementary teacher who already does a *superb* job of teaching early literacy skills? Or, if I am a science teacher who has been incorporating inquiry-based learning into my classes for years? In either case, it is very unlikely that I will benefit greatly by attending these workshops. Isn't there something else that I could work on to become a better educator? The simple answer to that question is "of course there is."

In contrast, the concept of "job-embedded" learning or professional development has the potential to be *much* more meaningful for educators at any level. The idea that professional learning is literally "embedded" within the scope and actual setting of an individual's classroom or school provides the potential for a much greater degree of professional growth. The reason is pretty simple: if you want to learn how to and what will improve learning for *your* students in *your* classroom, it only makes sense that *your* professional development should take place in and incorporate those specific parameters. To take something that is presented generically to a large group of educators—all of whom must go back to their classrooms and try to adapt and apply that which they have hopefully learned—does not seem to me to be an effective model. Ongoing, collaborative inquiry into what works in *your* classroom, *your* school, and *your* district, holds so much more potential for improved student learning, and for school improvement in general. In fact, in their original work, DuFour and Eaker (1998) stated the following:

> The most promising strategy for sustained, substantive school improvement is developing the ability of school personnel to function as professional learning communities.
>
> (DuFour & Eaker, 1998, p. xi)

I could not agree more. As you read more about the characteristics of PLCs, imagine these components at work in your school or district; imagine the *power* that they could hold for truly transforming the teaching and learning processes that occur in your settings. It is important to note that the term *professional learning community* has become commonplace, but the *practices* that truly represent a PLC are not the norm in educational settings (DuFour et al., 2008). In fact, I have personal stories that exemplify this fact. I have been in schools and

34 Professional learning communities

have overheard statements such as: "*Yes, we have PLCs in our school. We do PLCs every Tuesday morning from 7:30 to 8:30.*" I am not sure what they are doing every Tuesday morning, but they are certainly *not* "doing" a PLC. Faculty, staff, and administrators do not *do* a PLC; they *are* a PLC.

First of all, a PLC is not something you *do* for an hour a week. It is much more than simply sitting in the faculty lounge and having a conversation about a common educational topic. It is much more about a *way of professional life*, about the way you *approach* and *do* the job of being a professional educator, every minute of every day throughout the year. This is the primary reason that the notion of a *collective commitment* on the part of educators is so vital to the success and effectiveness of any school's PLC. When educators engage in a collaborative commitment to professional learning, it not only fosters professional learning in a community-type environment, but it also becomes an integral part of their daily professional lives. I believe that embracing the concept and characteristics of professional learning communities will forever change your lives as professional educators.

Next, we take a look at the six major characteristics of professional learning communities in greater detail. Please note that similar to some of the content in Chapter 1 of this book, the upcoming discussion is not meant to be an exhaustive presentation of the literature on professional learning communities. If the reader is interested in greater detail on PLCs, the reader should reference any or all of the following: *Professional Learning Communities at Work: Best Practices for Enhancing Student Achievement* (DuFour & Eaker, 1998); *Revisiting Professional Learning Communities at Work: New Insights for Improving Schools* (DuFour et al., 2008); *Learning by Doing: A Handbook for Professional Learning Communities at Work* (DuFour, DuFour, Eaker, & Many, 2006); and *Schoolwide Action Research for Professional Learning Communities: Improving Student Learning Through the Whole-Faculty Study Groups Approach* (Clauset, Lick, & Murphy, 2008).

Characteristics of PLCs

DuFour et al. (2008) list and discuss six characteristics, critical for the successful development and implementation of PLCs. These characteristics are:

Professional learning communities **35**

- A shared mission, vision, values, and goals;
- A collaborative culture with a focus on learning;
- Collective inquiry into best practices and current reality;
- An action orientation (or, learning by doing);
- A commitment to continuous improvement; and
- An orientation focused on results.

Next, we will look at each of the six characteristics individually, focusing our attention on their individual and collective contributions to successful professional learning communities in schools.

Shared mission, vision, values, and goals

The essence of any learning community is—and should be—a focus on and commitment to the learning achieved by each and every student under our charge (DuFour et al., 2008). There must be a shared purpose behind why we come to school each day. This shared purpose should be a driving force in executing the responsibilities that we collectively have. These collective commitments help clarify for the members of the PLC the exact contributions for which they are responsible. These shared foundational structures of a common mission (i.e., purpose), vision (i.e., clear direction), values (i.e., collective commitments), and goals (i.e., indicators, timelines, and targets) help educators by focusing *how* they will work to improve their schools. In addition, they collectively reinforce the moral purpose and collective responsibility that clarifies the reasons behind *why* their day-to-day work is so important— not only on the first day of school, but every day thereafter, as well (DuFour et al., 2008).

There are several important things to point out about these shared foundations of a PLC. First, time must be spent carefully crafting—using very specific terminology—the mission, vision, values, and goals. This is a critical fact. However, it may not be as critical as a second aspect: words alone—for example, writing and displaying a new mission statement or vision for your school—seldom impact how people act within an organization. Words on paper or on a banner for all to see are essentially useless unless the people in the organization begin to *act* differently (DuFour et al., 2006). This is truly where the part about *commitment* comes into play. Commitment to new missions, visions, values, and goals requires new actions on the part of everyone in the organization.

Third, the development of all of these shared entities requires a process of consensus building. "Consensus" does not mean that the mission, vision, values, and goals must be unanimously agreed upon by everyone in the organization; however, it does mean that each person in the organization is a participant in the process and has an opportunity to have his or her voice heard. This will go a long way in helping to create that sense of "sharedness" throughout the organization.

Collaborative culture with a focus on learning

A shared mission, vision, commitments, and goals make up the foundation of a PLC; a collaborative culture of teamwork then serves as the fundamental building block for a PLC in any organization. DuFour et al. (2008) have described this notion of collaboration as a collection of collaborative teams whose members work *interdependently* to achieve common goals. These goals must be linked to the overarching purpose of learning for each and every student. Furthermore, the members of the organization must be held mutually accountable for achieving those common goals.

A critical aspect of collaboration is that it will not lead to academic improvement unless people are focused—collectively focused—on the appropriate issues and goals. Collaboration is not the goal; it is a means to achieving the goal. In a PLC, collaboration is no more or no less important than the shared vision, commitments, and goals. They must go hand-in-hand; one must support the others, and vice versa. DuFour et al. (2008) have defined *collaboration* as "a systematic process in which teachers work together, interdependently, to analyze and impact professional practice in order to improve results for their students, their team, and their school" (p. 16). Clearly, this is no longer only about what happens in individual classrooms. It is much more about impacting and changing professional practice, so that students can realize improved academic performance.

Collective inquiry into best practice and current reality

This characteristic of PLCs is sometimes difficult for some teachers, as well as other school and district staff. Educators in a PLC regularly engage in collective inquiry into:

Professional learning communities **37**

1. Best practices about teaching and learning,
2. A candid clarification of their current practices, and
3. An honest assessment of their students' current levels of learning.

(DuFour et al., 2008, p. 16)

Number 1 in the list is not too difficult; however, Numbers 2 and 3 can sometimes create some discomfort among many professional educators.

A "candid clarification of current practices" requires a great deal of deep, meaningful professional reflection. It means being honest with oneself about things you do well . . . as well as things that you know you do not do well. Let's face it—as professional educators, none of us are perfect. There are things at which we excel in our respective classrooms and there are things that we know we could improve upon. The challenge here is to critically reflect and examine our own practices, which requires that we sometimes must be brutally honest with ourselves. If the overarching purpose of any PLC is to impact and positively change our instructional practices, we have to be willing to engage in this reflective process.

Similarly, developing an honest assessment of students' current levels of learning may often be seen as a reflection of our own capabilities, or perhaps, incapabilities. I liken this process to one where a person looks in a mirror, and engages in an honest discussion with the reflection about things that he or she does not particularly care for. It may not always be an easy thing to do, but it is a necessary component of being able to move forward in a positive direction. As professional educators, we cannot do this unless we know—clearly and honestly—the point from which we are starting.

However, in a PLC, the benefit is that *everyone* is engaging in this process of critical and systematic reflection and examination of student performance. Furthermore, having a collaborative support system can make these processes more manageable for many educators.

Action orientation: Learning by doing

Educators in a true PLC are action-oriented. They do not wait for things to happen to them or around them. They take the initiative;

38 Professional learning communities

they take the action to make things happen. These educators understand that the most powerful type of learning—both for themselves and for their students—will occur in the context of taking action. DuFour et al. (2008) describe this as being the very reason that educators should work together in teams and engage in collective inquiry, due to the fact that it serves as a catalyst for action, and ultimately for change. As an aside, this is probably my most favorite characteristic of PLCs—largely due to its similarity to and implied relationship with action research!

As educators, most of us would agree that hands-on learning typically results in the most powerful and meaningful learning for our students. Why should this be any different for us, as adults? In truth, it isn't any different. We learn better by taking a hands-on approach, as opposed to more minimal learning that results from reading, listening, or thinking. We all learn best by *doing* something, by taking action, by getting our hands dirty, so to speak. When we take action to do something, whatever we learn from the process will be more deeply ingrained in our experiences and in our knowledge base, not to mention in our skill set. This, in turn, serves as an impetus for positive change in our schools.

Commitment to continuous improvement

Inherent in the culture of a PLC is the constant search for better ways to achieve goals, for ways to achieve new goals, and to accomplish the overall purpose and vision of the organization (DuFour et al., 2008). There is typically a general sense of dissatisfaction among members of the PLC group with "keeping things the way they have been done in the past." This idea of dissatisfaction with the status quo and constantly looking for ways to improve engage each member of the organization in a systematic, ongoing cycle. (Hmmm . . . there appears another similarity to action research . . .!) This ongoing cycle includes:

- Gathering evidence of current levels of student learning
- Developing strategies and ideas to build on their strengths and address their weaknesses in learning
- Implementing the strategies and ideas
- Collecting evidence of the effectiveness of the strategies and ideas

Professional learning communities **39**

- Analyzing the impact of the strategies in order to discover what was effective and what was not
- Applying this new knowledge in the next cycle of continuous improvement

You can probably see why this is my second favorite characteristic of a PLC—note the similarity of the activities in this process of continuous improvement to the steps specific to the process of conducting action research that you read about in Chapter 1.

This commitment to continuous improvement encourages innovation and experimentation in our schools. For educators in a PLC, these activities are not viewed as additional tasks that must be completed; rather, they become the lifeblood of conducting day-to-day business in our schools and classrooms, for every member of the organization's PLC. This is the essence of professional learning through the application of action research.

Orientation focused on results

Finally, it is critical for educators in the PLC to realize that *everything* they do—from the development and implementation of their shared mission, values, and goals, to their collaboration, collective inquiry, action orientation, and focus on continuous improvement—must be evaluated in terms of actual achievements. In other words, making judgments about the level and quality of successes in a PLC based on *mere intensions* is not nearly good enough. The work of a PLC *must* be judged on the basis of *actual results* in terms of improved student learning and achievement. As DuFour et al. (2008) have clearly stated, "Unless initiatives are subjected to ongoing assessment on the basis of tangible results, they represent random groping in the dark, not purposeful improvement" (p. 17).

Note that the authors raise several important points in this brief comment. First, they state that the initiatives related to the work of a PLC must be subjected to *ongoing assessment*. If there is to be a focus on continuous improvement, then there must be a mechanism for continually assessing the extent to which targets are met and goals achieved. Second, they assert that *tangible results* must be assessed. If we truly want to know if our students' learning is improving, we must

40 Professional learning communities

assess specific results or measures of that learning. In Chapter 1 of this book, you read about the art of teaching—that is, "gut reaction instinct"—versus the science of teaching. Assessments of target achievements in a PLC cannot be based on gut reaction; this is the time for assessments of PLC initiatives that are grounded in "hard evidence," in the forms of data and other types of information about student learning.

Third, they assert that "groping in the dark" will not lead to *purposeful improvement*. When it comes to what actually works in education, in our schools, and with our students, I think we can all agree that "groping in the dark"—similar to "throw everything against the wall and hope that something will stick" and "let's run it up the flagpole and see if anyone salutes it"—is not an effective practice. Admittedly, there is nothing purposeful about any of these practices. Finally, I would add that the members of the PLC must have an open mind regarding efforts to continually assess the effectiveness of their efforts in terms of actual results, and must also be receptive to the results of ongoing assessments. The results and/or their assessments may not always be positive, but this is a necessary ingredient for determining what needs to be done in order to achieve the broad goals and vision of the PLC.

The challenge of a changing culture

By now, the potential rewards that can be realized from the implementation of a successful PLC should be obvious. So, why then doesn't every school and district become a PLC? The possible answers to that question are probably numerous; however, suffice it to say there is probably one major reason: implementing a PLC requires a huge change in the culture of a school or district. In fact, DuFour et al. (2008) have stated it this way: "It is impossible for a school or district to develop the capacity to function as a professional learning community without undergoing *profound cultural shifts* [emphasis added]" (p. 91). Not only must the change in the school's or district's culture be profound, it must also be *intentional*. The members of the PLC must intentionally facilitate these processes of cultural change. If this does not happen, it is unlikely that the culture will be positively impacted.

It is not uncommon for educators to erroneously believe that the types of change that should occur are those that resemble simple restructuring of various aspects of the school. Changing various structures within the school—for example, the daily schedule, the arrangement of student desks within classrooms, the layout of grade levels or subject area classrooms within buildings—will never be sufficient to create a functional PLC. It is not necessarily the case that these structures *should* not be changed; rather, the more important issue is that these types of restructuring activities may be necessary prerequisites for moving forward, but they will not serve as sufficient conditions to bring about forward movement, with respect to the vision and goals of the PLC. In the development of the foundational building blocks of the PLC—that is, developing the mission, vision, values, and goals—the members of the PLC may determine that these things are necessary and should happen. However, *only* changing these types of things will most certainly not result in the achievement of goals as established by the PLC teams.

The type of change that must occur is much more than restructuring; it is more appropriately broader, systemic change associated with *reculturing*. DuFour et al. (2008) describe *reculturing* as the challenge of positively impacting the assumptions, beliefs, expectations, and habits that constitute the norm within the particular school or district. When these efforts are successful, the school or the district becomes a very different place, where everything in the school looks, works, and functions differently than it did before the cultural change took place. The entire system, including everyone who works in it, will be required to do things and/or to do them in a way they have never been required to do before. As you can imagine, this will make some members of the PLC very uncomfortable. This is the true challenge of changing a school's or district's culture.

DuFour et al. (2006) identified several categories of cultural shifts that may occur in schools and districts in efforts to become a PLC, as well as specific examples within each of those categories. An adaptation of their list is presented in Table 2.1.

From this list, I think it is easy to see that many teachers—as well as many administrators—could be made to feel uncomfortable, perhaps even intimidated by the expectations of various changes in culture as a result of creating a PLC. However, to reiterate an earlier point—

42 Professional learning communities

TABLE 2.1 Categories and examples of cultural shifts that may occur in PLCs (adapted from DuFour et al., 2006)

Cultural shifts in a Professional Learning Community

A shift in fundamental purpose

From . . .	To . . .
A focus on teaching	A focus on learning
An emphasis on what was taught	A fixation on what students learned
Coverage of content	Demonstration of mastery
Providing teachers with state standards and curriculum guides	Engaging collaborative teams in building shared knowledge regarding essential curriculum

A shift in the use of assessments

From . . .	To . . .
Infrequent summative assessments	Frequent common formative assessments
Assessments used to determine which students failed to learn by an arbitrary deadline	Assessments used to identify students who need additional time and support
Assessments used to reward and punish students	Assessments used to inform and motivate students
Assessing many things infrequently	Assessing a few things frequently
Individual teacher assessments	Assessments developed jointly by collaborative teams
An overreliance on one kind of assessment	Balanced assessments
Focusing on average scores	Monitoring each student's proficiency in every essential skill

A shift in the response when students don't learn

From . . .	To . . .
Remediation	Intervention
Individual teachers determining the appropriate response	A systematic response that ensures support for every student
Fixed time and support for learning	Varying time and support for learning

continued . . .

Professional learning communities **43**

TABLE 2.1 *Continued*

A shift in the response when students don't learn . . . continued

From . . .	To . . .
Invitational support outside of the school day	Directed and required support occurring during the school day
One opportunity to demonstrate learning	Multiple opportunities to demonstrate learning

A shift in the work of teachers

From . . .	To . . .
Isolation	Collaboration
Individual teachers who assign priority to different standards, determine the pacing of the curriculum, and try different ways to improve results	Collaborative teams of teachers that establish priorities, agree on common pacing, and help each other to improve
Privatization of practice	Open sharing of practice
Decisions made on the basis of individual preferences	Decisions made collectively by building shared knowledge of best practices
An assumption that "these are my kids and those are your kids"	An assumption that "these are our kids"

A shift in focus

From . . .	To . . .
Independence	Interdependence
An external focus on issues outside of the school	An internal focus on steps the staff continue to improve the school
A focus on inputs	A focus on results
Goals related to the completion of projects and activities	Goals demanding evidence of student learning
Teachers gathering data from their individually constructed tests in order to assign grades	Collaborative teams acquiring information from common assessments in order to inform individual and collective practice, and to respond to students who need additional time and support

continued . . .

44 Professional learning communities

TABLE 2.1 *Continued*

A shift in focus . . . continued

From . . .	To . . .
A language of complaint and compliance	A language of commitment

A shift in professional development

From . . .	To . . .
External workshops, courses, and in-services	Job-embedded learning
The expectation that learning occurs infrequently and only on designated days	An expectation that learning is ongoing and occurs as part of the routine day-to-day work practice
Assessing impact on the basis of teacher satisfaction	Assessing impact on the basis of evidence of improved student learning
Learning by listening	Learning by doing
Presentations to entire faculties	Team-based action research

and at the risk of sounding repetitive—schools and districts can only begin to develop the capacity to function as a PLC once each member has made a conscientious and collective commitment to undergo profound cultural shifts throughout all aspects of the organization.

Reculturing any school or district is an extremely difficult task; no step-by-step process exists for altering the culture in an organization and that upon which that culture is built (DuFour et al., 2008). Even if one did exist, we would be hard-pressed to believe that it would work in every situation and setting. Therefore, you are left to your own devices to figure out how to change your own culture. However, this may not be a bad thing. After all, who knows your culture better than those of you who are immersed in it every day? The focus of reculturing a school or district is on changing people's behaviors. Many people succumb to the myth that you have to change people's attitudes before you can expect their behaviors to change. On the contrary, many scholars of educational and organizational leadership have written that only a change in practice—that is, behaviors—will result in a genuine

Professional learning communities **45**

change in attitudes, norms, and values. Leaders should focus their attention on first getting staff to *act differently*; however, a true transformation of the culture will not occur until new behaviors, practices, processes, and beliefs have become the new norm (DuFour et al., 2008).

Teaching and assessing in a PLC

Some of the most profound effects of becoming a PLC are the impact that it can have on the cyclical process of planning, delivering, and assessing instruction and learning. When compared to a more traditional school, the processes of planning and delivering instruction look very different in a school that operates under the foundational principles of a PLC. Below is a listing and discussion—some of which has been adapted from DuFour et al. (2008)—of several ways in which teaching has a different appearance, structure, and function in a PLC school.

- *Teachers no longer teach in isolation; collaboration is a fundamental key to the success of a PLC.* Within a collaborative teaching environment, no one is on his or her own; the "egg-crate" mentality has been abandoned. Each individual in the school—whether a teacher, staff member, or administrator—has someone, likely numerous people, to whom he or she can turn. Further, everyone has a colleague from whom they can learn on a regular basis. Instead of working *independently*, teachers work *interdependently* throughout all aspects of the teaching and learning process. Since everyone is operating within the same system of accountability, there are built-in checks and balances that help to ensure that everyone fulfills the expectation that each person contributes to the continuous improvement at their school. As the old saying goes, "there is strength in numbers."
- *The knowing-doing gap is bridged more effectively.* In the status quo model of teaching, the expectation for professional learning is that it occurs as a result of reading, coursework, and trainings and workshops. However, in a PLC that capitalizes on *job-embedded professional learning*, teachers gain invaluable knowledge as a result of their experiential "doing and learning." Much of this experiential, hands-on learning comes as a result of the complete avoidance of a sense of isolationism among teachers and staff in the school.

46 Professional learning communities

- *PLCs build shared professional knowledge and experiences, rather than simply pooling opinions.* One of the "unintended" benefits of becoming a PLC is that a school or district very quickly begins to build a "library" consisting of shared knowledge and experiences. Again, these shared knowledge and experiences are realized as a direct result of collaboration and job-embedded professional development. This occurs in direct opposition to a randomized "pooling of opinions" that typifies the status quo in a non-PLC setting. For example, gone are the days when you might overhear teachers say things such as "This is how *I* like to teach; *I* have always done it this way; I *think* it works for *me*." Instead, you are much more likely to hear teachers say—typically with a great deal of pride and confidence in their collective voice—"*We* know that this works for *our* students; let us show you the *evidence* we have."

- *Professional reflection becomes even more critical . . . and apparent.* Critical professional reflection is a key component in both action research and successful PLCs. In order for teachers and staff to successfully function as a PLC, they must engage in a high level of sound and critical professional reflection, during all stages of the teaching and learning process. This means that they must be critically reflective during the planning of instruction, the delivery of actual instruction, and the assessment of that instruction—and ultimate student learning. Like so many aspects and characteristics of a PLC, professional reflection becomes integrated into the day-to-day work of educators.

- *Teachers become vastly more empowered.* As you can see from the bullet points above, teachers begin to assume very different roles when they are engaged in a PLC process. They become much more empowered; they become leaders in their classrooms and schools. They begin to act much more like *professional educators* as opposed to simply "classroom teachers." Please understand that I do not mean to imply a negative connotation to the term "classroom teachers"; on the contrary, these teachers have in essence "stepped up their game," in order to act, behave, and work much more professionally than they ever have previously in their careers. Some may argue that teachers lose their autonomy in a PLC; I would argue just the opposite—in a PLC, and as part of a collaborative

Professional learning communities **47**

team, they have much greater power and have enhanced the likelihood that they will be successful for their students.

Similarly, processes related to the assessment of student learning appear much differently in a PLC school. I know firsthand from some of the research that I have conducted over the years (Mertler, 2005, 2009b, 2010) that assessing student learning—as well as assessment, in general—are not favorite topics for many teachers. They often believe that they have not received sufficient training in their undergraduate preparation programs, as well as in their graduate programs, in order to feel comfortable with their skills in conducting assessments and in making assessment decisions (Mertler, 2010). This is extremely unfortunate, in this day and age when so much is riding on accurate assessment of student learning, that so many teachers still view assessment as an afterthought in the teaching and learning process. Although we have seen improvements across the country in the past several years, many teachers and administrators could still be considered to be "assessment illiterate." There are those who still see assessment as nothing more than a mechanism for assigning grades at the end of the term. The view of assessment in PLCs is forcing this perception to change. Assessment in a PLC looks different than in a typical school. The following list, again partially adapted from DuFour et al. (2008), describes ways in which assessment differs in a PLC.

- *Formative assessment is the core of a PLC.* The focus of assessment in a PLC is to identify students who need additional time, as well as additional support, and to determine the specific content and/or skills where they need this support. Reliance on summative assessments—that is, those that are typically administered *following* large units of instruction and whose results are used largely for administrative purposes, such as assigning grades—simply will not accomplish this goal. Summative assessments are those that supposedly measure whether or not learning has occurred, after-the-fact. They are typically those that provide answers to questions such as: "A, B, or C?"; "pass or fail?"; or "proficient or not?" The use of formative assessments—that is, those that are administered *during* instruction and on a frequent basis, for the purposes of identifying gaps in instruction and learning that can be targeted

48 Professional learning communities

immediately—is aligned much more appropriately with the notion of helping to identify students who need additional *and timely* support. Formative assessments are effective at informing both student and teacher about a student's current level of achievement, as well as providing critical feedback to the teacher on his or her instructional practice so that timely adjustments can be made.

- *Formative assessments are commonly developed and administered frequently.* The notion of teams working collaboratively and building a shared "library" of knowledge and experiences is once again a central concept when we consider formative assessments in a PLC. These frequently administered formative assessments should be developed collaboratively by all teaching staff who are members of a particular team. When these *common* formative assessments are administered on a frequent basis, the members of the team—and the PLC as a whole—will have more confidence in terms of the extent to which progress toward the school's targets and goals is being made. Good teachers assess *all* of the time, and constantly use that assessment information to guide decisions about students and about their teaching.

- *Assessment is not used to reward and punish students, but rather to inform and motivate them.* Assessment begins to take on new meanings, not just for teachers, but also for students. Students learn to see the value in assessment, and how it can provide them feedback about their academic progress. I believe that they tend to fear, dread, and dislike assessments a whole lot less when formative assessments are administered frequently—not to mention the fact that they become less "stressed out" at the thought or anticipation of an assessment, as compared to situations where summative assessments were the norm and, if they did not perform well, results on those assessments became the source of punishment and perhaps even ridicule for the student.

- *PLCs stress a balanced approach to assessment.* When I teach assessment methods to preservice and in-service teachers, I am constantly stressing the importance of a balanced approach to assessment. Incorporating the use of multiple sources of assessment information can only make the decisions that we make about students more accurate. I urge teachers to use formative assessments—to do so when each is appropriate for the types of decisions that need to be made. I suggest that they use traditional test items, along with open-ended assessments and performance-based assessments. Teachers should also see the value in informal assessment methods, such as informal observations, frequent teacher questions, and even student journals. Once again, diversity in the types of information that we collect about student learning and about our own teaching will only help to make the decisions—as well as our progress toward our collective goals—more accurate.

Important takeaways from Chapter 2

- A professional learning community is a group of educators committed to working collaboratively in ongoing processes of collective inquiry action research to achieve better results for the students they serve.
- PLCs have a huge focus on collaboration, commitment, ongoing collective inquiry, and a focus on improved student achievement.
- Job-embedded professional learning is a key in professional learning communities.
- When done correctly, PLCs are not something that you do, they are something you become.
- PLCs share six critical characteristics: a shared mission, vision, values, and goals; a collaborative culture; collective inquiry; an action orientation; a commitment to continuous improvement; and an orientation focused on results.
- A PLC's action orientation, or learning by doing, creates a strong connection to action research.
- One of the most difficult aspects of implementing a PLC is the challenge of changing the culture in the school or district.
- Cultural aspects that must change include the foundational building blocks of a PLC, namely the mission, vision, values, and goals.
- The cultural shifts are far-reaching and include changes in the purpose of the organization, the use of assessments, what to do when students do not learn, the nature and work of teachers, professional development, and overall focus for the organization.
- Teaching looks much different in a PLC, where teachers collaborate, bridge the knowing-doing gap, build shared professional

50 Professional learning communities

knowledge bases, engage in critical professional reflection, and become more empowered.

- Assessment also looks different in the PLC: formative assessment is the focus, assessments are collaboratively developed and administered, assessments are not used to reward and punish students but rather to inform and motivate them, and assessments should represent a balanced approach.

3

THE ACTION RESEARCH MODEL FOR TRANSFORMATIONAL INNOVATION

In Chapter 3, I introduce and discuss a model for educational improvement that I developed several years ago (Mertler, 2011, 2013a). This model integrates several things that have been discussed throughout the previous two chapters of this book. The model itself is described, along with the five component parts. Finally, a discussion of possible applications of this model is presented.

What is the action research model for transformational innovation?

I do not believe that we have truly seen any effective large-scale reform in education over the past fifty years. In part, I attribute this to a lack of "oomph!" associated with terms like "reform," "change," "creativity," and "improvement." Calls for these types of movements are essential, but are no longer enough. If we factor out current advanced instructional technologies, the classrooms of today look very much like classrooms did when I was in school, over thirty years ago. Of course, there are exceptions to this characterization—for example, we are beginning to see teachers "flip" their classrooms, and use assessments in more constructive ways as positive approaches to student feedback. However, generally speaking, we have not seen drastic *across-the-board* types of reforms, changes, or improvements. Where is the true impact of large-scale educational reform? We need stronger language, and more influential movements.

52 The action research model

Let us take a closer look at some of these terms that we throw around in the name of educational improvement:

- "*Reform*" is formally defined as "the change or improvement of something wrong." Again, I do not believe that we have seen any effective large-scale *reform* in our educational system, largely because it is nearly impossible to pinpoint that which is wrong with it. There are not merely one or two things wrong; there may be a multitude of things wrong. Perhaps, more appropriately, there may be nothing *wrong*, but rather the interaction of the thousands of factors that can influence effective teaching and learning cannot possibly be isolated and targeted with interventions, without impacting numerous others.
- "*Creativity*" is defined as the occurrence of "something new being developed that has value to its audience." I think it has been a long, long time since anything truly new has been developed in education. In fact, what would something truly new look like?? We typically do not develop new things; we usually adapt, mold, and refine that which already exists into something that better meets our needs and the needs of our students.
- "*Improvement*" . . . hmmm? Is "educational improvement" something that we really need to talk about?? Shouldn't it be a given that we would *always* be trying to *improve* our practice?? It would seem that simple "educational improvement" is not an effective mechanism for pursuing positive—and meaningful—change in our classrooms. Its connotation does not really provide any "oomph" . . .

How many of us receive a new binder each August that outlines our new "reform" or "improvement" effort for the upcoming year? Talk about a bandwagon movement! This mentality that defines "reform" by handing out a new binder that defines the direction for the new school year is an outdated form of educator professional development.

In contrast, I believe that what we need in our educational system today is a *transformation* (defined as "a change or alteration, especially a radical one, to an existing entity") into something completely different.

The action research model **53**

Note in the definition that we are *not* creating some-thing new; instead, we are taking something that currently exists and effecting some sort of radical change to it ... radically changing how we teach something, how we ask students to demonstrate mastery of knowledge and skills, or how we structure our school day in order to facilitate professional collaboration, just to name a few.

In addition to engaging in a transformation of what we do and how we do it, we need to incorporate into that a mindset of *innovation* (defined as "a process that renews something that previously exists"). Often, what we do and how we do it as professional educators becomes outdated, or simply turns "stale." We need to breathe new life into it, energize it, revamp it—and perhaps, along with that, energize ourselves.

Notice how these two terms—*transformation* and *innovation*—exhibit a good deal of parallelism and, some might say, actually overlap. Both concepts focus on the idea of changing something that already exists. As professional educators, isn't this more realistically what we do? Therefore, I would like to provide a definition for a newly coined term: *transformational innovation*. I define transformational innovation as "the act of radically changing or renewing an existing system."

Additionally, I believe that we often think of large-scale innovations in education as a responsibility that belongs to someone else, whether it is the responsibility of researchers, policy makers, or legislators. We tend not to think of these kinds of things being done at the grassroots level. The true benefit of engaging in this process of transformational innovation is that it empowers educators at all levels to design, implement, and evaluate innovations at a grassroots level, and to learn and grow from engaging in this type of professional experiences. This becomes much more powerful than "typical" professional development for educators.

My process of transformational innovation in education consists of the integration of five key components, all centered on action research at its core. A visual depiction of the component parts of the model is presented in Figure 3.1. This model can serve as a guide for educators— everywhere and at all levels—to engage in a process of action research for the purposes of (1) improving their own particular practice and (2) designing and implementing their own job-embedded professional

FIGURE 3.1 The action research model for transformational innovation (Mertler, 2011, 2013a)

development. Each of the component parts of the model is discussed in the next sections.

The five components of the model

The Action Research Model for Transformational Innovation is an integrated model comprised of the following five components:

- Data-driven educational decision-making;
- Data, data, and more data;
- Thinking differently;
- Collaboration; and
- Professional reflection.

The five components should not work, nor should they be considered, in isolation. It is critical that implementation of this model reflects an integrated approach, not only factoring in all five components, but also centered around *action research* as its core facilitating mechanism.

Data-driven educational decision-making

Over the past decade, we have seen a dramatic shift in what we have come to expect from our teachers. For many years, the best teachers were those who could truly make decisions "on the fly," using gut instincts. Earlier in this book, this is what I have referred to as *the art of teaching*. However, in this age of accountability, the art of teaching is no longer enough. We are now beginning to see a comprehensive shift to an equally important skill set, that which I like to call *the science of teaching*. The art of teaching is essential; the science of teaching is critical.

The science of teaching centers around decision-making based on evidence (i.e., data). The art of teaching versus the science of teaching is not an "either-or" proposition; the concepts of teaching as an art form and teaching as a science *must work in unison with one another*. The science of teaching is a much more systematic, scientific approach to decision-making; it is a more systematic process of trial-and-error. When you truly adopt such an approach to your professional work, I believe that you have developed a mindset of *data-driven educational decision-making*, or *D-DEDM*, for short.

Generically speaking, this more scientific approach looks like this:

Generate an idea
↓
Implement the idea
↓
Assess its effectiveness
↓
Reflect on the process

It very closely parallels the process of *action research*, as we examined earlier in Chapter 1. Recall that in Chapter 1, I presented a cyclical four-step process for action research:

56 The action research model

Planning for your action research

↓

Acting on the plan

↓

Developing an action plan for future cycles

↓

Reflecting on the process

It is critical for you to see the similarities in the process of conducting action research with those of a more generic process for D-DEDM. In each of the above processes, the second and third steps involve two critical activities on the parts of educators:

- The second step involves the collection of data; and
- The third step involves making decisions based on those data.

There are two key pieces about this component of our discussion of the action research model for transformational innovation in education that I think are vitally important to raise at this point:

1. This process is context-specific; more importantly, it is specific to *your* context. *You* plan for *your* action research. *You* are investigating what's important to *you*, in *your* classroom, for *your* students, with respect to *your* instruction—have I made my point that the focus is on *you* and *your* context!!?? In my opinion, there is no better way to customize your own professional development than to focus your attention on the following question: What do *you* want to improve in *your* classroom? Status quo, one-size-fits-all professional development does not accomplish this.

2. Once you have results from your action research inquiry, you can take action immediately. After all, it *is* your classroom, etc. More traditional forms of educational research do not facilitate this type of immediate professional action, this type of meaningful data-driven educational decision-making.

At this point, you are getting closer to being able to engage in your own systematically derived, data-driven educational decision-making. As classroom educators, how many of you have truly experienced this kind of empowerment? I firmly believe that the process represented by the overall model *truly empowers* educators by providing a mechanism for job-embedded professional development—growing and developing in areas that *you* deem important to *your* professional practice.

Data, data, and more data

Historically speaking, as educators, we have had a narrow and limited view of what constitutes data in our systems of data-driven educational decision making. As recently as a decade ago, these data were largely limited to those resulting from the administration of standardized tests. I do not subscribe to this extremely limited perspective on data. I explain my stance this way:

> I honestly do not know anyone who loves standardized testing! But, the standardized testing movement is not going away anytime soon. An examination of its impact on this country's educational system over the past 40 years will confirm that. Therefore, I approach it from this perspective . . . and I strongly suggest that all professional educators adopt a similar attitude. Any time we are given the responsibility of making decisions about children, we need as much information as possible in order for those decisions to be as accurate as possible. We ask students questions; we ask them to read to us; we require them to write for us; we test them over units of instruction; we observe them; we encourage them to be creative; we engage them in perform-ance-based tasks; etc. The results from standardized tests are just another source of information—about student learning, about our teaching, and about our curriculum. Please use them as such—add them to your long list of various sources of infor-mation about student learning. They can only help improve the accuracy of the decisions that we make about our students, as well as our own instruction.
>
> (Mertler, 2007, p. xii)

Interpreting standardized test scores has not always been an easy task for classroom teachers; however, it has improved. However, I would argue that there are no real limits to what we can use as sources of evidence to help inform our decision-making. Schools are *full of data*! As a brief, partial list of examples of sources of information that

58 The action research model

generate both summative and formative student data that can be used to inform our decision-making, we can make judicious use of any or all of the following:

1. Summative assessments:

   - teacher-developed tests
   - performance-based assessments
   - standardized test scores

2. Formative assessments:

   - diagnostic assessments
   - informal assessments (e.g., questions, observations, minute papers, and muddiest point exercises)
   - surveys and inventories
   - student journals
   - teacher journals
   - reflection papers
   - interviews
   - etc., etc., etc.

When we are charged with making decisions about children, we need as much information as possible in order to make accurate decisions. The potential negative consequences of inaccurate decisions are just too overwhelming, too risky, and way too costly. I urge you not to limit yourselves in terms of what you use to help inform your decision-making processes.

Thinking differently

In order for us to successfully design and implement transformational innovations in education, we have to be willing (and able) to *think differently*. What we really need is some *ultra-creative* brainstorming! We need ideas for how we can move the educational process forward—especially in our own classrooms, schools, and districts—taking those ideas and integrating them into our overall process for utilizing an action research approach to collect a variety of data in order to make well-informed data-driven decisions, and move our profession forward. What I am referring to is not just "thinking outside the box." I think that

The action research model **59**

term has become overused, and it just does not have meaning anymore. Just consider—if we are all thinking outside the box, is anyone really *outside* the box anymore? I think that the box has merely gotten bigger, and now encompasses all "non-traditional" thinkers.

At the risk of dating myself, I must admit that I love the old Apple marketing campaign from 1997 (which you can view here: www.youtube.com/watch?v=tjgtLSHhTPg). In that video, actor Richard Dreyfuss, as the narrator, talks about the "crazy ones," "rebels," and "misfits," and how those individuals thought differently. They were not afraid of what others thought of their ideas, because *they believed in themselves*. Where would we be today if those individuals had not shared and acted on their different, but very forward-thinking, ideas?

Pull out some chart paper and colored markers, grab your dry erase markers and make a beeline for your whiteboard—nothing is "off the table." We cannot be afraid to throw out ideas, no matter how "different" they might seem at the outset. You never know what may develop from an idea that you might have been previously hesitant, or even afraid, to offer. Now more than ever, we need some "crazy ones," some "rebels," and a few "misfits"—educators who are willing to not only think outside the box, but perhaps *live* outside the box (!) and give us their ideas for transforming the work of educating our nation's children.

Collaboration

I believe that the fourth component in my action research model of transformational innovation in education is a key component, if incorporated properly. Quite simply, collaboration enables us to accomplish so much more than pursuing these kinds of innovative initiatives single-handedly. However, it does require a shift in mindset.

First of all, as you have read earlier in Chapter 2, collaboration requires us to abandon the "egg-crate mentality" that many of us were either taught or have just adopted (or fallen into) over the years. We need to step outside the four walls of our classrooms and collaborate with peers and colleagues. Second, bringing together different perspectives, experiences, and ideas provides us with opportunities to develop our ideas more comprehensively. We can "pick and choose" aspects from a variety of sources and a variety of ideas to come up

60 The action research model

with a more widely agreed-upon plan of action or potential solution to our problem. This of one of the real advantages of collaborative brainstorming sessions. However, there is a potential downside—that not all ideas may be adopted. Then, of course, personalities can come into play, sensitivities arise, and feelings may be hurt. These types of things have to be addressed, but if they are addressed from a professional perspective, they can have positive outcomes.

Third, working together toward a common goal can be extremely powerful, and effective. The sense that we are not trying to accomplish something that may, at times, feel overwhelming single-handedly can actually be refreshing. We need to trust our fellow educators, and feel that, by "pooling our resources," we stand to accomplish so much more. Finally, I also believe that collaboration can provide opportunities for practitioners and researchers/consultants to work together, but also have the sense that they are working together (as opposed to the researcher/consultant guiding what the practitioners do).

Two concepts that lend themselves very nicely to these ideas of collaboration are *professional learning communities* and *collaborative action research*. Each is valuable in its own right, but they also share a good many characteristics that can prove invaluable to this process of developing and implementing transformationally innovative ideas in education. You have already read a good deal about collaboration in PLCs—you know what the experts say, and that I agree. Let us then take a look at collaborative action research.

There are several key characteristics of *collaborative action research* (Clauset, Lick, & Murphy, 2008, p. 2), which you will undoubtedly see as being quite "parallel" with concepts we have discussed regarding PLCs:

- *Collaborative action research consists of practitioners working together as a team.* Again, this is just the notion that a group of educators has adopted more of a team mentality. The success of the team has much greater significance that the successes of any one individual.
- *The focus of the team is on a common issue, problem, or goal.* The key word here is "common." All members of the team must agree on the purpose and the target of the collaborative work.
- *There should be the development of a synergy that inspires one another.* Once this synergy begins to develop (and it may take some time),

The action research model   **61**

the team will feel as if nothing can stop them from achieving their collective goals.
- The focus should be on creating momentum toward more insight into the problem, and greater learning and growth relative to the common issue being examined by the team. I believe that it is so much easier to create this kind of momentum when several people are "pushing," instead of all of us trying to do it on our own.

I think that you can probably see the connections and parallels between the concepts of collaborative action research and professional learning communities. There really is no reason to "go it alone." There is strength in numbers. Collectively, we can accomplish so much more. If you have not already done so, go out and forge collaborative working environments today; I really do not think that you will regret it.

Professional reflection

I think that the fifth, and final, component in my action research model for transformational innovation is the glue that holds the model together. There is a good deal of overlap and parallel between and among various aspects of these five components, but I believe that professional reflection really runs throughout the model. I define *professional reflection* as a process whereby educators critically examine their own teaching methods, etc., in order to determine what is most effective for their students. Like so many things that we have throughout this book, the true value is that the collective focus of these efforts and initiatives is on *your practice*.

If you think about the processes that we have examined previously concerning D-DEDM and action research, they are, by nature, reflective processes. One of the true benefits of these reflective processes is that they provide wonderful opportunities for educators to essentially customize their own professional development. You engage in a process, seeking answers to your questions about your own practice, your own students, your own instruction, etc.:

- How do I currently teach my students these skills and concepts?
- How will I teach this differently next time?

62 The action research model

- Should I sequence it differently?
- How should I effectively assess my students' mastery?

Professional reflection fosters a level of professional learning that is highly valuable, primarily because it is personalized, and therefore very meaningful. As you know, we have not been able to get this from the "one-size-fits-all" model of professional development.

In addition, professional reflection should be ongoing. If it is properly incorporated into the model for transformational innovation (i.e., it is integrated into the processes of D-DEDM and action research, as well as into a process of collaboration and as a mechanism for thinking differently), reflection never really ends. It is an ongoing aspect of the iterative cycle of this systematic and scientific critical examination of our own practice.

Reflective practice is difficult for some educators because it forces us to look inward, to be introspective, and to be honest with ourselves. We are trying to look at what we have done in the past—and how our practice looks in general—in order to determine what we do well, as well as areas where we need to improve. Reflection is not an aspect of professional practice that should be taken lightly; it is a *critical* part of professional growth and learning. Combined with the other components in a cohesive model, you have a sound process for engaging in professional development, learning, and growth.

One additional (sub)component . . .

So, what happens when we engage in this process of transformational innovation, and we end up being wrong? Perhaps not a formal component, but certainly an additional key aspect of the model is that *we must be willing to make mistakes, to learn from those mistakes, and to continue to strive for movement forward.* Being wrong and making mistakes is not bad; we simply need to be willing to take those occurrences, learn from them, and use them constructively in the future. Elizabeth City (2010) has echoed these sentiments:

> One of the limits to our current approach to goals, measuring, and accountability is that it rewards cautious behavior. When the stakes are high and we're not sure what to do, we try lots

The action research model **63**

of little things in the hopes that some might be right and none might be wrong. [We need movements that inspire] innovation and experimentation, but only if it makes it OK to be wrong sometimes. We must be willing to be wrong or we will never achieve greatness. . . . In education, the fear of failure leads to many things; one of the most important is lack of imagination. This matters because there is a powerful connection between imagination and hope and [between] hope and action.

(p. 63)

We cannot afford to be cautious any longer, especially if we are doing so in order to avoid failure. In Seth Godin's (2011) book, *Poke the Box*, the author discusses the act of "poking the box," or taking action, taking initiative, and taking risk. Specifically, he says:

Risk, to some, is a bad thing, because risk brings with it the possibility of failure. . . . [For] some, risk comes to equal failure. . . . Risk is avoided because we've been trained to avoid failure. (p. 14)

Poking doesn't mean right. It means action. (p. 42)

When the cost of poking the box is less than the cost of doing nothing, then you should poke! (p. 29)

Change is powerful, but change always comes with failure as its partner. "This might not work" isn't merely something to be tolerated; it's something you should seek out. (p. 44)

Not engaging in transformational innovations is far worse than doing so and being wrong! If you cannot fail at something, is it really worth even trying?

In one of his famous TED Talks, Sir Ken Robinson (2006), international expert on creativity, said:

If you're not willing to be wrong, you'll never come up with anything original.

64 The action research model

I might also add that if you're not willing to be wrong, you'll never come up with anything *meaningful*. We do not have to wait for innovations to filter down to us, to our schools, to our classrooms. The model of action research for transformational innovation in education is a mechanism for *educator empowerment*. Take the initiative and move your professional practice forward!

Implications of the action research model for transformational innovation

So, at this point in our discussion, some of you might be asking: "The action research model looks an awful lot like professional learning communities; what's the difference?" Admittedly, there are some similarities—in both, there is a general dedication to a common set of goals, a focus on using data and other sources of information, and a commitment to a collaborative culture. If you revisit Chapter 2—and the characteristics that comprise PLCs—you will see that action research is included, specifically as part of the "action orientation" component of a PLC. Recall that I discussed what I see as a *minor* degree of overlap between action research and PLCs. Suffice it to say, action research is *present* in a PLC. However, I do not believe that it is a *major* focus in a PLC. In fact, you will read in Chapter 4 of this book the ways in which I envision an *action research community*, and how it compares to a PLC.

However, I think the main difference between the action research model for transformational innovation and a PLC is the fact that action research is at the *core* of the model for transformational innovation. In other words, everything that happens within the model for transformational innovation all comes about as a result of *educators committing to continuous improvement through frequent and sustained action research*. The impetus for school improvement *is* action research itself. I firmly believe that *action research serves as the catalyst for job-embedded, customizable, and meaningful professional development*. The fact that action research is the central, driving force within the model makes this an incredibly strong model for school improvement and professional growth.

Important takeaways from Chapter 3

- Transformational innovation is the act of radically changing or renewing an existing system.
- The process of transformational innovation in education consists of the integration of five key components, all centered on action research at its core.
- The five components of the action research model of transformational innovation are: (1) data-driven educational decision-making; (2) lots of—and wide varieties of—data; (3) thinking differently; (4) collaboration; and (5) professional reflection.
- The five components should not be treated separately, but rather should be integrated throughout the model.
- Data-driven educational decision-making is, in essence, the science of teaching; it incorporates a systematic, scientific component into the process of decision making.
- There should be no real limits to the amount and types of data used to aid in data-driven educational decision-making.
- Thinking differently is not just about thinking outside the box, but perhaps also *living* outside of the box; it should be integrated into all aspects of the professional work of educators.
- Collaboration encourages us to abandon our "egg-crate mentality" and work together in professional teams toward common goals.
- Two concepts that lend themselves to professional collaboration include professional learning communities and collaborative action research.
- Collaborative action research is characterized by: (1) educators working together as a team; (2) the focus of the team is a common problem, issue, or goal; (3) the development of an inspirational synergy; and (4) a focus on professional growth and learning as related to the common problem or goal.
- Professional reflection is the critical self-examination of one's teaching practice, with the goal of improved student learning.
- In applying the model, educators must be willing to make mistakes, to learn from those mistakes, and to continue a momentum toward enhancing professional practice and improved student learning.
- The action research model for transformational innovation in education is somewhat similar to the concept and practice of a PLC.

66 The action research model

- Action research is the core of the model for transformational innovation.
- Within the model, action research serves as the catalyst for job-embedded, customizable, and meaningful professional development for educators at all levels.

4

PUTTING IT ALL TOGETHER

Action research communities

The concept of action research communities is introduced in this section. The discussion focuses, in part, on the extension of PLCs through the growth and expansion of action research within the PLC framework. Included are presentations of how action research communities should function, as well as the various roles for teachers, building administrators, and district administrators.

TI-*in*-ed + PLC = ARC

I have had this idea for some time, but it really came to the forefront as I finished teaching an online graduate-level course in action research a couple of years ago. For one of their last assignments, I asked my students—all of whom were classroom teachers earning Masters degrees in various areas of education—to share their thoughts about action research and whether they would continue to conduct their own action research studies, outside of their coursework. The students unequivocally stated that they believed there was a huge value and benefit to designing and conducting their own action research studies. However, with so many other duties and responsibilities, most felt that they would not have the time to engage in such professional endeavors. I understand—trust me, I truly get it—but I think that they might be missing the bigger picture in all of this.

I "get it" because, to a degree, I think they are right. While I believe that conducting action research in isolation can still be hugely beneficial, doing so leads to a feeling of, well, isolation. To be honest—none of us really wants to do anything if we feel isolated in doing it.

68 Putting it all together

However, I believe that so many of those "other duties and responsibilities" could be enveloped in an action research approach and mindset. Additionally, we need a supportive environment; a *culture* that promotes, values, and rewards professional activities that result in us *becoming better educators.* Please do not misunderstand me—as I said earlier in this book, I know that doing this requires time, resources, and commitment. But, by implementing much of what has been discussed throughout this book, you can collectively capitalize on so many aspects of what you are undoubtedly trying to do in your schools.

What I am really talking about is the development of *action research communities*, or *ARCs*. An action research community takes all that is professionally beneficial from the action research model for transformational innovation and combines it with all that is beneficial from the concept of a professional learning community (see Figure 4.1). An ARC is a PLC; however, *the driving force behind an ARC is that action research serves as the overarching focus, the mechanism that drives a faculty and staff to its common mission and vision, and the common thread that provides the foundation for collaborative teamwork and professional growth.*

Specifying the purposes and functioning of an ARC

My vision for ARCs is that they operate similar to any other PLC, with all the essential components (e.g., a shared mission and vision, collaboration, collective inquiry, an action orientation, a commitment to continuous improvement, and an orientation focused on results). The only real difference is that the focus, mindset, and *culture* are all based in and are created around *collaborative action research in your schools*. In other words, the commonality shared by all participants in the ARC is the fact that they engage in collaborative action research for the purposes of improving their practice and ultimately improving student learning.

As I have mentioned earlier, one of the distinctive benefits of action research and collaborative action research is the opportunity for educators to *customize their own professional development*. When a PLC is structured around collaborative action research at its core— thus, making it an ARC—not only is there a common vision for school improvement, but also educators are permitted to pursue school improvement that is geared toward *their own identified areas* for

Putting it all together **69**

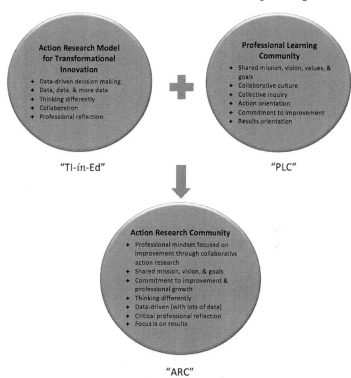

FIGURE 4.1 Conceptual diagram of an action research community (ARC), combining the model for transformational innovation and characteristics of a professional learning community

professional growth and advancement. I do not believe that there is an existing structure—even for PLCs—that provides educators these sorts of customizable opportunities.

Of course, this customization of professional development does not have to be different for every individual in the ARC. The benefit of a school- or district-based ARC may not stop at the simple implementation of action research studies that are specific to each individual participating in the ARC. For example, ARCs can foster collaborative action research that include all teachers in a particular content area, department, or grade level, or that crosses disciplines, grade levels, and

70 Putting it all together

perhaps even school buildings. Can you envision just how powerful could this be in your schools?

According to DuFour, DuFour, and Eaker (2008), a PLC's mission, vision, values, and goals form the *four pillars* of that learning community; they are the *foundation* upon which the learning community is built. If we consider the foundational structure of an ARC—that is, *its* mission, vision, values, and goals—we find the same basic structural importance. The only variation that one might see is the fact that the action research component is an integral piece of these four pillars. A new, ARC-driven mission statement must move beyond simply focusing on the fact that "everyone should learn," and rather should embrace a *new focus*, an orientation on *new actions*, and a commitment to reflective inquiry. If the purpose of a school or district mission statement is to answer the question "*Why do we exist?*", then an ARC mission statement should not only focus on high levels of student learning, but also the means by which that will be achieved—in other words, improvement in student achievement through *an applied, context-specific approach to professional development through action research*. A hypothetical example of a mission statement for an ARC might read as follows:

> It is the mission of our school to provide every opportunity for our students to learn at their highest levels of capability, through engagement in a continuous process of reflective inquiry and action research, in order for our educators to grow professionally in a manner that focuses specifically on the academic, social, and emotional needs of our students.

Admittedly, there may be aspects of that mission statement with which some of you disagree; however, please notice the focus on the integration of continuous reflective practice and action research as necessary actions to be taken by the educators who are focused on achieving this particular mission.

The power that lies in the implementation of ARCs is potentially immense . . . perhaps even limitless. Admittedly, their implementation requires some degree of planning and coordination. However, I firmly believe in them, and in the fact that their potential benefits far outweigh their initial "start-up costs."

Putting it all together **71**

Roles for teachers in ARCs

Mind you, designing and developing—and ultimately implementing —a culture appropriate for an ARC is not necessarily an easy task. It requires educators to embrace *reflective practice*. It requires a serious reexamination of long-held professional belief systems. It requires a hard look at the various roles traditionally held by teachers and those by students. There may be some fear, some hurdles, some barriers, perhaps even some failures along the way. However, I believe that expressing— and embracing—this type of courage can be its own reward. Journeys of this magnitude require commitment on the parts of *courageous professional educators*—those not afraid to step outside their comfort zones, not afraid to critically examine their own practice, and not afraid to make the occasional mistake (but to also learn from it at the same time).

In an action research learning community, planning time, collaboration time, and professional development are not crammed into a thirty- or sixty-minute time slot at the *end of the day* or *first thing in the morning*. The commitment requires an "all day, every day" attitude toward professional growth, development, and learning. The ARC mentality should be integrated into everyday practice; it should become *indicative* of how teachers do their jobs . . . *every day*. Teachers must commit to investing *real* time to truly collaborate and to substantially improve their practice. This becomes a fabulous opportunity for teachers to be able to focus their attention, in a collaborative manner, on methods of improving their practice. Let us collectively raise the profession of education back to a status of a *true profession*—a profession where we:

- recognize our professional limitations,
- work collaboratively to improve them, and (as a result)
- make the lives of the students and families with whom we work better, more productive, and more successful.

In order to accomplish this, one of the things that I think must happen is that educators everywhere, and all levels, must be willing to adopt a mentality where research guides our practice. In order to do this, teachers must embrace the "inner researcher" that lies within each of them. Let me provide you with five reasons why I believe that this is critical:

72 Putting it all together

1. *It is risky to rely on the research of others.* For a couple of decades, we've been inundated with folks telling us that the potential solutions that we seek for our classroom and schools need to be "research-based." As a trained educational research methodologist, I completely agree. However, I also want to make you aware of several limitations of relying on research-based solutions:

   - *Timeliness.* When you find an empirically based research article, keep in mind that (depending on the journal or other publication) the actual research may have been done anywhere from one to three years earlier. It is typical that it may take this length of time for a researcher to get a manuscript published. You *may* be making a decision about your instruction or curriculum based on research that is essentially outdated.

   - *Generalizability.* For those of you familiar with research terminology, you know that this refers to the likelihood that the findings from a given research study will "translate" equally well to your setting. In other words, remember that the study in question was *not* conducted by studying *your* curriculum, *your* school, *your* students, or *your* teaching style. Why, then, should it naturally follow that the positive findings resulting from that study will also carry over to your setting with equal success? I would argue that it should not naturally follow; at a minimum, one should review the study very carefully prior to simply implementing its procedures.

   - *Appropriateness or fit.* Often, published research studies have goals that are broader than the specific types of questions we might have about our own students and teaching. While that particular research might "loosely" fit our needs, it really does not provide a good fit to our immediate goals. To me, this is akin to wearing popular loose-fitting shorts or t-shirts— sure, they meet the general need (i.e., they have place for your legs and arms), but they are way too big and just do not provide an appropriate fit.

2. *You can customize your research findings.* As I have discussed numerous times throughout this book, action research—and the action

research model for transformational innovation—provide a structured mechanism for customizing your research findings in order to enable you to address your specific questions or concerns in your classroom, school, or district. The best way to know if something will work with *your* students or in *your* classroom is to try it out, collect data to assess its effectiveness, and then make a decision about your next steps. Why would you want to try to answer your questions or solve your problems about *your* students and *your* teaching with *someone else's* methods and data?

3. *You can experience the feeling of empowerment.* It is critical to realize that what I am advocating is not just the fact that you can implement solutions on your own, but rather that you can also take the lead in designing those solutions in the first place. Take the initiative to become the empowered professional educator that you are capable of becoming.

4. *You can investigate your own practice.* Think about this for a moment—all the hours of preservice teacher coursework; the hours of graduate coursework; the countless hours of in-service workshops and trainings—have you ever wondered if all that "stuff" you learned was actually working in your classroom? Why not investigate your own practice as a means of discovering what works and what might not be working as well as you had hoped. The clear benefit of doing so is that you begin to add the "science of teaching" to your educational repertoire, in addition to what you know and practice about the "art of teaching." This is data-driven educational decision making in its purest form.

5. *You can impress others at dinner parties.* How many times have you experienced the uncomfortable line of questioning and comments at a dinner party. You know—"Teachers have it easy. You only work 9 months each year. You get off of work at 3:00 each day. How hard can it be? You work with kids all day." The next time you encounter such antiquated thinking, share with your dinner colleagues the new research that you are conducting with your students, the new and innovative things you are trying, and the successes you are experiencing. You just might impress them!

Finally, the idea of collaboration extends beyond simply working with one another to also *supporting* one another. Professional support

74 Putting it all together

can be incredibly powerful and life-changing for many people. Just because you are not working directly with one of your colleagues does not mean that you are not capable of serving as a support mechanism, a sounding board for ideas, or simply a shoulder to lean on when things might get a little tough. Even if individual teachers might never take advantage of those support systems built in to an ARC, knowing that they are there and available—if and when they might be needed—can be highly influential in terms of changing and sustaining a new cultural mindset in a school.

Roles for building administrators in ARCs

As with any PLC, principals and assistant principals in an ARC take on key roles in terms of its success. In these situations, the best leaders are those who respond to the complex demands—not only those of their position, but also those specifically of the action research learning community—by reducing the plethora of challenges to a handful of crucial aspects that can permeate throughout a school (DuFour, et al., 2008). Principals and assistant principals must lead by example. They must determine what the *essential aspects* of their positions are and demonstrate to the faculty and staff in the school how to focus on the most critical needs at a particular time.

Within an ARC, building leadership must focus on the level of overall commitment to fostering and promoting the necessary change in culture. Further, the leadership must focus on sustaining this commitment throughout the faculty and staff. Focusing on the school's mission and vision—all while leading by example—is paramount in sustaining these types of efforts. Faculty and staff in the school must know and see—on a daily basis—that the principal and assistant principal(s) are equally committed to the overall success of the learning community and that they will be supportive of faculty and staff needs. When teachers know that they have logistical and emotional support from administrators and their colleagues, it can be a huge and influential factor in the success of school improvement efforts throughout a building. How meaningful would it be to know that a principal, for example, encourages and supports teachers making their own attempts at figuring out how to promote innovation by developing and implementing alternative teaching strategies?

A few years ago, I worked closely with a school in Birmingham, Michigan, at the request of the building principal. The particular school was a science and technology school for grades 3–8, and the principal invited me to come to the school and spend a day working with the entire staff to begin developing a mindset for the implementation of innovation using an action research approach, and to do so using a learning community mindset. The principal and assistant principal challenged their teachers to individually or collaboratively design and implement their own action research projects, in an effort to target self-identified areas in need of improvement. I continued to work with them in a consultative role throughout the school year. However, the one aspect of their approach that I think was highly influential was the fact that not only did the principal and assistant principal *support* their teachers' efforts by providing them with appropriate time and resources, but they also designed and conducted *their own* action research project, examining their professional communication style within the school setting, in an attempt to find out what worked and what did not work, and to target ways to improve their professional communication style and efforts. The fact that they joined in this empowering innovation mindset—*alongside their teachers*—still impresses me to this day. They have continued to build and sustain the action research community that they began that year; it has become part of their culture, and professional support has been a big piece of that. True transformational innovation in education takes time. Support is a necessary ingredient for the successful implementation of innovative ideas. The unknowns are scary—and failure or mistakes may be a real possibility—but you have got to get out there and go for it, supporting each other in the process.

Roles for district administrators in ARCs

If the proposed ARC is to be a district-wide effort, then district-level administrators play an essential role, as well. They must be able to promote and facilitate not only enhanced student learning, but also improvements in adult learning. In other words, they must be the ambassadors for a shift in culture that promotes a new model of professional development for faculty and staff in the district. They must be able to emphasize the importance of reflective practice and self-guided inquiry into context-specific teaching and learning.

76 Putting it all together

DuFour et al. (2008) recommend the following four keys for shaping a new culture within a PLC—and, specifically within an ARC:

1. District leaders must capitalize on every aspect of an effective change process in order to present a compelling rationale for moving forward. Persuasive strategies might include any or all of the following:

    -   Providing sound reasoning and rational thinking
    -   Sharing existing research
    -   Providing influential "arguments" that resonate with the faculty and staff
    -   Re-situating data into cases focusing on the human element of teaching and learning
    -   Providing necessary resources, in addition to a system of rewards
    -   Highlighting and sharing real-world success stories
    -   Making compliance a requirement

    District leaders can provide the necessary culture-shift leadership by influencing the motivation of each individual in the organization, enhancing the personal abilities of others, making beneficial use of positive peer pressure, capitalizing on the relative "strength in numbers," developing a system of rewards, expecting accountability, and altering the organizational environment in order to support the change.

2. District leaders must communicate the priorities of the learning community effectively and consistently. Everyone in the action research community should be held to the same expectations and standards. When a district leader is willing to compromise, or negotiate, with certain individuals in the district, an extremely negative mixed-message will resonate throughout the entire organization. The message—that is, the mission, vision, values, and goals—that is shared must be communicated consistently day after day.

3. District leadership must be strategic in terms of limiting comprehensive initiatives in order to allow for the sustained focus necessary for an ARC initiative. If this does not happen, the simple result is a lack of coherence, focus, and commitment. People will

Putting it all together **77**

simply feel that their attention is being pulled in multiple different directions on a daily basis. As you can imagine, when this occurs, initiatives die quickly due to a lack of sustainable efforts.

4. District leaders must help school personnel build a collective capacity to achieve their missions by embedding ongoing professional development as a routine part of the job of being a professional educator. As you read earlier in Chapter 4, as well as in Chapter 3, one of the major focal points of the action research model for transformational innovation and of action research communities is the fact that job-embedded professional development is an ongoing and sustainable type of initiative that is integrated into the concept of an ARC. If an ARC is implemented as designed, the concept of job-embedded professional development is not only automatically built in, but that type of professional development is also—theoretically—individually customizable for each individual in the learning community.

For me, this is the bottom line: comprehensive change initiatives—like designing and implementing an ARC—will never be sustainable and effective without the support, driving influences, and leadership by example that comes from both the district and building levels.

Important takeaways from Chapter 4

*   An action research community (ARC) is a professional learning community where action research serves as the overarching focus, the mechanism that drives a faculty and staff to its common mission and vision, and the common thread that provides the foundation for collaborative teamwork and professional growth.
*   The focus, mindset, and culture of an ARC are all based in and are created around collaborative action research in schools.
*   One of the benefits of collaborative action research is a capacity for educators to customize their own professional development.
*   Within an action research community, educators are permitted to pursue school improvement efforts that are geared toward their own identified areas for professional growth and advancement.
*   The foundational structure of an ARC should not only focus on improving student learning, but also the means by which those

78 Putting it all together

improvements will be realized—that is, through an applied, context-specific approach to professional development through action research.

- Successful ARCs require that teachers embrace reflective practice and an "all day, every day" attitude toward professional growth, development, and learning.
- Reasons for embracing your "inner researcher" include: it is risky to rely on the research of others; you can customize your research findings, investigate your own practice, and gain a sense of empowerment.
- Professional support is an integral part of an ARC.
- Building- and district-level administrators must lead by example in an ARC, in order to gain the support and commitment of the entire organization.
- Building- and district-level administrators must present an ongoing, compelling rationale for initiative focusing on this type of forward movement.
- Building- and district-level administrators must deliver a convincing and consistent message—both verbally and non-verbally—when communicating about an ARC.
- When implementing an ARC, the predominant focus for both school and district initiatives should be centered on the comprehensive success of the action research learning community.
- The success of an ARC is contingent on the delivery of a compelling message and argument in favor of job-embedded professional development as a routine part of the job of being a professional educator.

5

WHERE DO WE GO FROM HERE?

Sustaining and growing your ARC

In this section of the book, we will take a look at ways in which ARCs can be extended. In other words, these are strategies for ways to sustain the action research community, foster the cultural shift that accompanies the implementation of an action research community, and grow the impact and importance of the action research community. Several strategies are presented in Chapter 5; however, the reader is encouraged not to limit these efforts to only those discussed here. This may be an opportunity for creativity to shine, and for further innovation to germinate.

Ways to sustain ARCs

As with any type of professional learning community, a legitimate challenge is that of trying to put things in place that will help to sustain and grow the impact of the learning community. One of the worst things that can happen is to start off the implementation of any learning community with a full head of steam, only to see the interest, passion, and commitment wane and potentially disappear in years two or three. Several things can be done to sustain the initial momentum created in an action research community (Dufour, DuFour, & Eaker, 2008; Dufour, Dufour, Eaker, & Many, 2006). These strategies include the following:

- Whenever feasible, *link* reform efforts to *current practices* and *existing assumptions*.

80 Where do we go from here?

- Focus first on the *why*, then on the *how*.
- Work diligently to align *actions* with *words*.
- Be flexible on *implementation*, but firm on the essence of the *reform initiatives*.
- Build a strong guiding *coalition*, but do not wait for unanimity.
- Expect to make *mistakes*, but also expect to *learn* from them.
- Continue to learn by *doing*.
- Strive for *short-term victories* . . . and *celebrate* those victories.

Link reform efforts to existing practices

Simply put, educators will be more inclined to support the focus of an action research community when it is presented as "evolution" rather than "revolution" (Dufour et al., 2006). Reform efforts, cultural change, and innovations should be connected to existing practices, principles, and assumptions. It should be presented to—and, therefore, perceived by—members of the ARC as a natural progression of ongoing efforts to improve academic achievement, as opposed to something completely new and different that the school/district is trying out.

Focus on "why," then on "how"

As you have read and will read more about later in this book, implementing an ARC is a process. However, it is a process that must be preceded by guiding and overarching missions, visions, and values. It is incredibly important to possess a firm understanding of *why* you are engaging in this action research learning community journey before diving headfirst into the proverbial icy pond of *how* we will accomplish this change initiative. The logistics of *how* must be linked to the *why*, as represented by the articulated purpose of the school and/or district. Educators (i.e., participants in the ARC) must see the explicit linkages between these two entities in order to make firm commitments to its purpose and goals. Maintaining a focus on *why* we are doing this—throughout the life of the action research community—may actually be more critical than focusing on *how* we are doing this (especially since the *how* may develop, change, transform, and/or metamorphose, over time).

Align actions with words

Capitalizing on the need to keep a focus on *why* the work of the action research learning community may be necessary, it is critical to ensure that the *actions*—on the parts of both leadership and participants in the ARC—are continuously and consistently aligned with the words that are guiding the work. Of course, these words exist in the form of the mission and vision statements. Therefore, it is essential that the actions of leadership reflect those statements that are designed to guide the work and to delineate the goals of the action research community. Actions—including communications—must be focused on and directed toward these goals. When they are not, these actions tend to detract from the clarity, consistency, and collective nature of the work being undertaken by the learning community. Educators participating in the ARC are then being presented with "mixed messages" about the initiatives within the school, as well as how those initiatives will be achieved and the target goals met.

Be flexible, but firm

It is important to remember that there is no single correct way to lead an ARC; similarly, there is no single way to accomplish the work and goals as set out in the ARC. Therefore, it is crucial that all of the members of the action research learning community maintain some degree of flexibility when it comes to implementing initiatives as a means for achieving the goals. Where there can be no flexibility is on those aspects that drive and direct the work, namely the guiding mission and visions. Leadership must remain firm on the guiding principles and the essence of the change initiative.

This, in essence, becomes an issue of keeping a focus on the "big picture." There may be tendencies for leaders in an action research community to "cut corners," for example, to agree to proposals from educators to compromises that might expedite the overall process and work of the ARC. While at the time, and on the surface, this may not seem like a catastrophic decision, Dufour et al. (2006) are quick to remind educators that the most common cause of the demise of a professional learning community initiative tends not to be the result of a single cataclysmic event or decision, but rather is the result of

82 Where do we go from here?

repeated compromises to the fundamental and foundational principles of a learning community. There typically is no single fatal blow; action research learning communities tend to die out from repeated small wounds over the course of time. This, alone, is the main reason for remaining firm on that which serves as the core of the action research learning community.

Build a coalition, but don't wait for unanimity

There are two important aspects of this particular tactic for sustaining action research communities. First, it is important for leaders to realize that they cannot do this type of comprehensive work alone. It is important not to lose sight of perhaps the most important keyword in the descriptor of our initiative—that is, *community*. Action research learning communities—as with any professional learning community—require the active involvement and support of numerous people. It is critical for leadership to build consensus and commitment among many individuals within the school. When it comes to action research learning communities, this not only means consensus and commitment toward being part of a *learning community*, but also possessing a commitment to the potential power and benefits of engaging in regular classroom- and school-based *action research*.

However, a second important aspect of this tactic is that leadership should avoid the tendency to wait for unanimity before moving forward. The bottom line is that, if one waits for unanimity, one should be prepared for an incredibly lengthy wait before getting started—most likely, an *endless* wait and *complete failure* to get started. While we would like to think that everyone in the school would be "on-board" with our reform and change initiatives, we simply know that this will not be the case. Individuals will have concerns, and the best thing that leadership can do is attempt to address those concerns. However, halting the implementation of an action research learning community in order to convince a handful of holdouts may become a completely counterproductive activity. A more effective tactic might be to begin the work of the action research community, as a means of demonstrating to the naysayers how meaningful it can become. This will likely result in many of them wanting to join the positive and proactive efforts represented by the ARC. In fact, when I conduct action research workshops and trainings for schools, I often use the graphic below:

~ Start a ripple effect in your school ~

I am a firm believer in the fact that these kinds of initiatives in schools can begin to take on lives of their own. As a small group of educators begins to work proactively on improving their own practice—as well as the school as a whole—the impact can begin to have a ripple effect across the entire school. In some cases, a slow and leisurely ripple effect may begin to take on an uncontrollable and infectious sort of spread throughout the school.

Expect mistakes . . . and learn from them

Whenever we engage in this kind of comprehensive work, we know that there will be mistakes. My personal perspective on this is that mistakes are nothing more than invaluable learning opportunities. Earlier in Chapter 3 of this book, I shared a quote by Sir Ken Robinson (2006):

> If you're not willing to be wrong, you'll never come up with anything original.

I also added to that quote by including that "you'll never come up with anything *meaningful*." Not only is it important to *expect* mistakes, but I believe that it is vitally important to be *willing* to make those mistakes. The difference is that people who merely *expect* mistakes typically do not know what to do when they are confronted by a mistake that they have made. In contrast, people who are *willing* to be

84 Where do we go from here?

wrong and to make mistakes seem, to me, to be slightly more "advanced." They have a predisposition, of sorts, to actually *welcome* the mistake, primarily because it gives them the opportunity to engage in professional reflection, to critically learn from that mistake, and move forward in a much more proactive manner. When members of the action research learning community adopt this fundamental shift in mindset, the ways in which a school—along with its change initiatives—can progress are seemingly limitless.

Learn by doing, not by additional training

As with many new initiatives in the broad field of education, there is typically the misconception among educators that engagement in some sort of new endeavor or activity requires a good deal of formal training in whatever those processes entail. Simply engaging in professional development sessions does not automatically result in the transference of skills from a "learning" situation to a "doing" situation. Most of us know that if you truly want to learn how to do something, you must actually do it—and not just read about it or sit through a presentation on it. Most of us would probably agree that we learned more about the teaching profession during the first semester of our first real teaching job than we did in four or five years of sitting through courses in a teacher preparation program.

Action research learning communities require an orientation based in *taking action*. Learning how to function as a professional learning community, or learning how to conduct an action research study—by reading a book or simply being trained to do such—proves to be a set of ineffective strategies, if individuals do not *actually* participate in a learning community or *actually* conduct their own action research studies. Learning by doing will often result in mistakes along the way; however, these mistakes can prove to be so much more enlightening (see the previous section above) than if one was to simply sit through a three-hour workshop on the topic.

Of course, there may be some preliminary knowledge to which members of an ARC might need access. However, this does not require hours and hours or days and days of additional training *prior* to beginning the implementation of an ARC. Oftentimes, the *will* to engage in these kinds of activities far outweighs the *skills* that one might possess. Additionally, ARC training may be most valuable when it is delivered as individuals are engaged in doing the actual work of an ARC (Dufour et al., 2008). Finally, keep in mind that one of the driving forces behind an action research learning community is its collaborative nature; our colleagues are there to help us when we encounter struggles or hurdles along the way.

Short-term victories . . . and celebrations

Action research communities often get off to a very strong start, but then somewhere in the middle, interest begins to wane, change efforts do not seem to proceed smoothly, or initial goals and timelines may seem unrealistic. When these types of events occur, it is crucial for all members of the ARC to remember that initial efforts to implement change and reform do not represent the final outcome. First and foremost, the work of an action research learning community is a *process*.

This is one of the main reasons that action research lends itself so nicely to the concept of a professional learning community. Action research is a cyclical process; it does not represent a "once-and-you're-done" set of procedures. It is best to think of it as repeated sets of trial-and-error processes. Blending action research with the professional learning communities concept necessitates a *sustained effort* toward comprehensive school improvement and increased academic achievement. One of the keys to a successful action research learning community is how people—and, in particular, school leaders—respond to mistakes or failures, and then how long they can sustain their efforts in the face of these types of adversities (Dufour et al., 2008).

Unfortunately, human nature often dictates that we focus our energies on the negative occurrences in our lives. It is sometimes difficult to "stay the course" when dealing with these mistakes, failures, or other types of difficulties and challenges. Success in an action research community must rely on altering these natural tendencies, and attempt to focus the bulk of our energies on the successes that are undoubtedly occurring. One idea to help educators refocus these energies on the positive is to "create" short-term victories. My use of the word *create* is not meant to imply some sort of falsification of successes, but rather the intent is to search for positive aspects of things

86 Where do we go from here?

that may otherwise be seen as failures or shortcomings. As the old saying goes: *every dark cloud has a silver lining*. As members of an action research learning community, we have a responsibility—as well as a debt to all of the other members of our collaborative learning community—to seek out, recognize, and otherwise identify the positive aspects of our collective work, and to identify them as victories or successes. *I believe that it is critical that we look out for one another, in an attempt to ensure that no member of the community begins to focus or to dwell on negative aspects or outcomes associated with the ARC.* Even in situations where we may deem our action research study to have been a "failure," I can almost guarantee that you will have learned something beneficial through engagement in the process.

That being said, however, I do not believe that simply identifying or recognizing these small victories is enough. We collectively owe our colleagues the right—and, quite frankly, the *opportunity*—to celebrate these victories, no matter how small they may be. Every educator involved in the action research learning community is taking a risk, to some degree. Each person has put himself or herself "out there," trying new things and perhaps not having any idea what the outcomes might be. For most of us—again, dictated by human nature—this can be an extremely uncomfortable position in which to find ourselves. We *need* the collective support; we *deserve* the collective support. It is positively crucial to the success of the action research learning community that our victories be recognized *and* celebrated, as a learning community. We need to feel that what we are doing matters and is making a difference. Having the support and commitment from our action research learning community colleagues is crucial to its overall success and longevity. These victories and subsequent celebrations help to foster both the passion and persistence within our learning community.

Ways to extend ARCs

It is important not only to *sustain* the work of an action research community, but it is also extremely important to engage in activities that will *grow* and *expand* its impact. This can be accomplished in numerous ways. However, one of the things that you will notice about these various activities is that they all tend to increase the *empowerment of educators* involved in the action research community. Several of these types of activities upon which I will expand include the following:

- *Technology* can be utilized to extend and grow your network of collaborative professional educators engaged in action research in schools.
- ARCs can also be used to *engage students* in the teaching and learning process in new and innovative ways.
- ARC efforts could be supported through *grant funding*, bringing additional financial support to your district.
- *Mini-grants* could be awarded to your educators who actively participate in ARC activities.
- Continued support through the provision of various *incentives* can also help sustain ARC efforts.
- Activities associated with the ARC might be incorporated into your *personnel evaluation system*.
- Eventually, you could sponsor an annual or bi-annual *conference* to showcase the innovative work in which your educators are engaged. This could, perhaps, even be extended to include educators in neighboring districts.

Integrating technology

In today's globally connected, technology-driven world, professional educators have abilities to create enormous and meaningful networks of potential collaborators. Often, when we think of being part of a learning community, I think we tend to focus on a community that is defined only by those individuals with whom we can gather in the same room. Unfortunately, this is a limited view of *any* sort of professional learning community, but especially of ARCs. When considering potential problems of practice that might serve as a focus for action research—or, perhaps, even an entire ARC—I think that it is important to consider that fact that there are likely educators elsewhere in the country or even the world who might be experiencing similar challenges in their classrooms or schools. By finding and connecting with these educators—and making them part of your ARC—you only increase the generation of ideas, innovation strategies, methodological ideas, etc., for your action research.

88 Where do we go from here?

Technology can serve as the means of connecting these extended ARCs. I tend to stress the use of tools that encourage professional collaboration. Video conferencing applications such as Skype or Google Hangouts can be downloaded and used free-of-charge. These are immensely helpful in terms of being able to facilitate synchronous connections between people anywhere in the world. There are, of course, numerous other video-conferencing software and web-based applications that you might choose to use, if your organization already has a subscription to those services. Other web-based applications like *Google Docs* for documents (www.google.com/docs/about/), *Google Sheets* for data spreadsheets (www.google.com/sheets/about/), and even *Google Slides* for presentations (www.google.com/slides/about/) can aid collaborative work within ARCs. You can even create surveys for data collection with *Google Forms* (www.google.com/forms/about/).

Geographic proximity—or lack thereof—should never limit ways in which we connect, collaborate, and innovate with other professional educators. The list of ideas presented in the previous paragraph is but a brief list of possible ways to utilize technology to coordinate and facilitate your work in an action research community. I strongly urge you to reach out to your fellow professionals and connect with them to address your problems of practice, collaboratively design and implement new teaching and learning strategies, and innovate in your schools and districts.

Student engagement

Students' voices—in addition to their engagement in the entire research process—can play an important role in ARCs. Over the past several decades, the teaching and learning process has become much more student-centered. Much of what we do in classrooms and in schools directly affects our students. Students play a vital role in terms of letting us know what they believe is and is not working for them. Therefore, student engagement in various phases of the action research process could provide essential feedback to the success of an intervention or innovation in our classrooms and schools.

Student engagement and involvement in action research might look very different from project to project. For example, student input might be used to generate new potential activities that could be used in a class to support extensions of learning. Similarly, following a pilot test for a new intervention strategy, a small group of students could participate in a focus group discussion to provide immediate and invaluable feedback on the effectiveness of the strategy. After all, it would be important—and much more time efficient—to gauge what might need revising prior to widespread implementation of the specific strategy. Finally, imagine doing some sort of collaborative action research on school climate—we would certainly want to include student voice in that project!

The true value in engaging students in different ways in an ARC is that they begin to develop a greater sense of ownership of their learning, and of the content being taught to them and the way it is being taught, supplemented, assessed, etc. I certainly do not mean to imply that students should have the same degree of opinion and level of judgment and decision-making that other members (i.e., teachers and administrators) of the ARC may have; however, they may be able to provide insight into the impact of a new intervention or instructional technique that other educators may not be able to see, due to the fact that it comes from *their* perspective, and not ours. This is a highly valuable perspective that we should not take lightly, and must be willing to include in the process in order to make an ARC as effective as possible.

Grant funding

As we all know, there are lots and lots of grant opportunities out there that can help support various educational initiatives in our schools. Before you spend a lot of time looking, let me assure you that it will be difficult for you to find grant opportunities that specifically address action research in schools. While I personally would love to find some to help support these types of initiatives, I have looked and—generally speaking—they do not exist. However, I would strongly urge that you not let this discourage you.

On the plus side, action research in classrooms and schools has begun to grow immensely over the last decade. Interest has increased, along with active participation in terms of engagement in the action research process. Educators across the country are beginning to see the real impact

90 Where do we go from here?

that action research can have on the quality of the teaching and learning process, student academic growth, educator professional growth and development, and overall school improvement. While there may not be grants available that specifically target the use of action research, there is absolutely no reason the action research cannot be a driving force, instrument, and/or strategy embedded in any grant proposal that targets some other aspect of the teaching and learning process.

If you were to do a quick search of grant funding currently available through the U.S. Department of Education (which I did in order to obtain the list below), you would likely find grant-funded programs that might address—but certainly would not be limited to—the following categories:

- reading
- the teaching of math
- preparation for success in post-secondary education
- teaching American history
- the development of innovative magnet schools
- innovative solutions to common educational challenges
- STEM education
- elementary and secondary counseling programs
- and, the list literally goes on, and on, and on . . .

The important thing to note here is that regardless of the topic or the nature of the grant program itself, action research—and more importantly, action research learning communities—can be extremely effective in implementing and investigating any and all of the above-listed grant program topics. More specifically, incorporating action research into grant proposals provides opportunities for educators to utilize a formal process for purposes of investigating new strategies, instructional techniques, instructional support materials, and student assessments, all through the use of student and teacher data collected through a systematic process of action research.

Mini-grants to ARC participants

Due to budget cuts and shrinking resources across the board, one of the things that I think we are beginning to see more of in our school districts is financial support from local businesses. It is not uncommon to drive past schools and see banners hanging out front listing local businesses and organizations that have provided a variety of resources to that particular school. One approach that could be utilized to support an action research learning community might be a system where teachers, or collaborative groups of teachers, could request mini-grant support from one or more sponsoring businesses or organizations. I would anticipate that there would be businesses and other organizations that might have a great interest in providing relatively small amounts of financial resources to support innovative work being done in their local school districts.

In contrast, this type of mini-grant program would not have to be funded solely by local business. It could actually be incorporated into a much larger grant proposal. This way, the funding to support the mini-grants to teachers and other educators would not have to come from private businesses, but could be included as a specific line item in the grant proposal budget. Of course, incorporating this type of support system would require some additional resources—primarily in terms of time (e.g., for reviews of mini-grant proposals, etc.). However, the benefits could be immense, since more teachers might be willing to actively participate in the ARC, knowing that they would have some financial support for their efforts (at least, in terms of costs for additional materials, equipment, technology, etc.).

Systems of incentives

It is important to admit that most of us did not enter a career in education for the vast amounts of money that we would make. On the contrary, most of us did it because of the intrinsic rewards attached to the teaching profession. However, that being said, I do believe that structures need to be put in place to *incentivize* this kind of professional development and work. These incentives could exist in the form of extrinsic rewards (perhaps, a grant-funded stipend, gift cards donated from local businesses, or prime parking spots), or in the form of recognition efforts (such as a recognition dinner, or a school- or district-wide "innovation conference" where educators "show off" and share the work that they have been engaged in). This last idea will be discussed in more detail in a moment.

92 Where do we go from here?

When presented with the concept of committing to an action research learning community, educators often struggle with finding the time necessary to engage these professional activities; they must be provided with the appropriate time to do this kind of work that we have discussed throughout this book. Time is an issue for all us in our places of work. For many teachers—who truly *value* engaging in this kind of work—*availability of time, itself, is an incentive.* The bottom line, from my perspective, is that time must be created, carved out, set aside. There needs to be designated time to work on these sorts of transformational efforts. This can be accomplished through common planning times, designated teacher work-days (or half-days), or perhaps periodic "professional retreats," where meetings and collaborative work might take place off-campus, away from the distractions of our everyday work. Time is a precious resource if we truly want to innovate in our schools and classrooms.

Another incentive—although we may typically not think of it as an incentive—is to provide teachers with the appropriate resources to help them engage in this type of work. Once again, when it comes to action research, many teachers are admittedly extremely uncomfortable with the thought of designing and conducting their own research studies. I believe that part of this problem stems from the fact that numerous methodological and procedural decisions must be made at the outset of the study, as well as during the course of conducting the study. In an effort to help teachers and other educators engage in this decision-making process related to designing and conducting action research, I have developed templates, in the form of interactive PDF files, called the *Action Research Mentor Portfolio* (Mertler, 2015). The *Action Research Mentor Portfolio*—available at Teachers Pay Teachers (www.teacherspayteachers.com/Product/Action-Research-Mentor-Portfolio-2285854)—assists professional educators, as well as individuals in other professions, in designing action research studies for their particular settings. If important methodological and procedural decisions are not made carefully and thoughtfully, there could be unexpected negative ramifications later in the study. The *Action Research Mentor Portfolio* provides guidance to help educators make sound decisions—before, during, and after conducting the action research study. Focused questions and prompts guide the user through this decision-making process. Interactive templates are organized by the

Where do we go from here? **93**

four stages of action research (as previously shown in Figure 1.2), and include the following specific aspects of the action research process where the user can obtain direction and mentorship:

The Planning Stage

- The 5 Why Process for Problem Identification
- Organizing Your Literature Review
- Developing a Research Plan

The Acting Stage

- Planning for Data Collection
- Planning for Data Analysis

The Developing Stage

- Action Planning

The Reflecting Stage

- Reflecting on the Action Research Process

Classroom- and school-based action research

Professional reflection

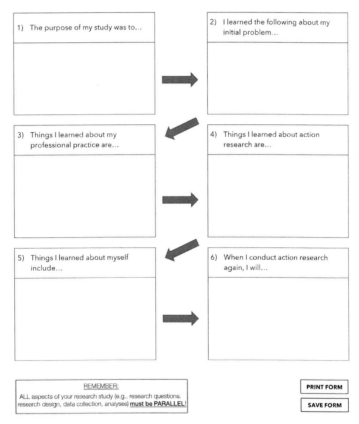

© 2015 by Craig A. Mertler, Ph.D.

FIGURE 5.1 Example template from the *Action Research Mentor Portfolio*

An example of the template for "Professional Reflection" is shown in Figure 5.1. In addition, all of the templates are provided in the Appendix.

Once the user has answered the questions and addressed each prompt, "pages" can be printed or emailed (for example, to a professor, advisor, supervisor, or administrator). You can purchase and download the interactive templates from TeachersPayTeachers.com for $1.50 USD.

Engaging in work and ideas that are transformationally innovative is difficult, challenging work; however, the short-term and long-term benefits vastly outweigh the challenges. But, if we are going to expect professional educators to engage in and commit to a collaborative action research learning community, then we need to be prepared to treat them like the professionals that they are, and reward their professional efforts and accomplishments.

Components of personnel evaluation systems

Increasing accountability measures are currently fueling the debate regarding the most appropriate way to measure teacher effectiveness—and to reward teachers for doing excellent work. At the risk of adding more fuel to the fire, I am willing to argue that a "one-size-fits-all" model of teacher evaluation—based, at least in part, on standardized test performance—may not be the best system.

Further, I would argue that a much more appropriate system would be one that incorporates the action research model for transformational innovation in education *and* action research learning communities, allowing educators to customize *their* own professional development, focusing on specific aspects of *their* teaching that *they* want to and need to improve. This could then serve as a basis (at least, in part) for their annual teacher evaluations.

For example, educators would begin the school year by developing specific professional development goals for themselves for the year. Now, please note that these should not be the kinds of goals that I was required to submit prior to each school year back in my high school teaching days. I was required to complete a form listing three goals for myself at the beginning of each year. Here is the problem with

96 Where do we go from here?

that—I was *never* held accountable for achieving *any* of the goals that I listed. If we permit educators to develop their own professional development goals, and to systematically collect data and investigate their own practice, we need to hold them accountable for the degree of their successes (or at least for what they learn as a result of engaging in such a process).

By doing so, they have greater ownership over—at least part of—their annual evaluations. And, I would venture to guess that they would take more pride in what they choose to investigate about their own practice since the focus was *theirs* (unlike when the focus is on the test performance of their students). They are responsible for collecting their own data, which comes from their actual work in their own classrooms, and typically not from standardized tests (although test data could be used). These data could also include student feedback or student evaluations of teaching (SETs), which provide a voice for students in the process, as well.

Arguably, this is a potentially unique approach to teacher evaluation, especially in today's educational climate. However, how much more would educators buy into this type of evaluation process? I think they would do so at a much higher instance. This would also potentially solve the problem of evaluating teachers who teach in non-tested areas—they still have classrooms with students, and are able to target areas in need of improvement. Also, this could open the door for other teacher evaluation possibilities. Imagine groups or teams of teachers "transformationally innovating" to solve an issue common to their classrooms, subject matter, or specific course. The result could be collaborative, or group, teacher evaluations. Think about this for a moment . . . *we expect teachers to work together, but we evaluate them as individuals*. Does that make sense???

I have said it before, and I will say it again . . . we need to treat educators like the professionals they are, and to allow them to utilize their expertise and resources to improve their own practice. Then, we can truly hold them accountable for the work they are charged to do. This system, including the processes and mechanisms discussed throughout this book as a means for development of a collaborative commitment to teacher-led action research, provides us with a mechanism for doing so.

Action research/innovation conferences

I want to revisit one of the components in the action research model of transformational innovation; that of professional reflection. Reflection is a critical piece to the overall effectiveness of action research learning communities, and of action research in general. It is about learning from the critical examination of your own practice, but also about taking the time to critically reexamine exactly who was involved in the process, what led you to want to examine this aspect of your practice, why you chose to do what you did, where is the appropriate place (time, sequence, location, etc.) to implement future changes, and how this has impacted your practice. Taking the time to thoroughly answer these kinds of questions for yourself will aid in an even deeper, more meaningful examination of practice, as well as a heightened level of empowerment.

However, this is still not enough to fully gain an appreciation for professional reflection on the critical examination of your own educational practice. In order to take your reflective activities to a higher level, I strongly encourage educators to:

Share . . . Disseminate . . . and Celebrate!

Let me share my thoughts about each of these individually.

First, I believe that it is incredibly important to *share* the results of critical examinations of your practice with colleagues in your schools and districts. There are multiple reasons for doing so. Many of your colleagues—because they may teach the same curricular content, standards, learning outcomes, or students—may have a great deal of interest in finding out what you discovered from examining your own practice. For example, if you developed and implemented a successful new supplemental activity to reinforce your students' learning, they might want to try it as well. This type of sharing can be done informally at grade-level meetings, school-wide faculty meetings, or even at school or district-wide *action research conferences* or *"innovation conferences,"* as I like to call them. In an attempt to make them somewhat less intimidating, these action research or innovation conferences can be set up to encourage informal presentations of the results of action research projects. An example of a poster—designed

FIGURE 5.2 A sample poster presented at a research conference

to engage the presenter and audience in informal discussions about the study—presented at a similar conference is shown in Figure 5.2.

Also, by sharing your professional work and results, you also encourage others to engage in these types of activities in their own classrooms. I have worked with countless teachers who have said that they simply do not know how to do these types of things, or simply do not have the time. Seeing colleagues with whom they work successfully carry out action research studies might just encourage them to try it as well. Educator empowerment can be contagious!

Second, while I feel that it is important to share these outcomes locally, I also firmly believe that it is crucial to *disseminate* your work within the larger educational community. This is most easily done by presenting your work at professional conferences. Again, this is typically something that teachers and administrators are not very comfortable with, but I would encourage you to "think outside your *local* box," and give it a try. Remember, if you are collaborating on your reflective and innovative work, those collaborations could—and should—also extend to professional presentations. However, do not feel that you

Where do we go from here? **99**

have to start really big by presenting at a national conference (although that will certainly get the word out about the innovative work you're doing!); rather, start at a more comfortable level by presenting at state or regional conferences. Also, the related benefits that can come from networking and idea-sharing among new colleagues can become incredibly valuable.

Third, engaging in these types of truly professional activities is something that you should truly *celebrate*. Please do not lose sight of the fact that this is a BIG deal! You are empowering yourself to take charge of a situation in your own professional setting. You are not waiting for things to "filter down" from educational research or from your state department of education. *You* are taking the lead on finding ways to do *your* work better and more effectively. Take time, find ways, and collaborate to celebrate these professional successes. As I mentioned earlier, a great way to do this is to hold school- or district-wide conferences where educators from all levels (teachers, administrators, counselors, etc.) present their critical and professional examinations of practice to peers. This can be done very efficiently as a poster-session type of conference, allowing for an informal setting of professional conversations.

While you may see some overlap or parallels among these three reflective activities, I encourage you to engage in all three. They each provide you with unique opportunities to engage in professional communications with peers (both local and non-local), to network, and also to recognize and commemorate your innovative action research reflective inquiry.

Implementation of an ARC represents a *process*

It is critical to remember that the action research model of transformational innovation in education is a *process*. The thing about any process—such as the one that we have been discussing—is that it can develop into a highly *individualized* process. Depending on the topic you are investigating—using an action research approach, relying on data-driven educational decision-making, based on wide varieties of data, working in collaboration with your colleagues in your classroom or school—you might need to adapt the process into various nuances of the original in order to meet your needs. It is important

100 Where do we go from here?

to realize that this is a perfectly acceptable practice. The process of engaging in classroom- and school-based action research is designed to offer a good degree of flexibility. The basic structure of the process remains, but it is critical to see it as an *iterative* process, as opposed to a linear (i.e., step-by-step) process.

So, then, how do you get from where you currently are to where you want to be (i.e., *more innovative, thus transforming your practice through applied action research*)? How do you get yourself and other educators motivated to engage in a process that can literally change the way you approach your work as professional educators, possibly for the rest of your careers? How do you encourage educators to take on these challenges . . . challenges that can change how and what students achieve? Further, how do you sustain it, keep it going, year after year? I believe that this is best accomplished through a well thought out infrastructure to support transformationally innovative work in our schools. Three of the most important features that are necessary requirements for this infrastructure are:

- providing the necessary time and resources,
- encouraging a culture of collaboration, and
- including rewards or some other type of recognition.

Finally, it is important to remember that implementation of action research learning community represents a process, and a nonlinear one at that. There will undoubtedly be struggles, hurdles, and challenges along the way. However, I firmly believe that implementing a professional learning community with action research as its central, core focus will result in academic and scholastic outcomes that will positively impact your professional practice for the remainder of your career.

Important takeaways from Chapter 5

- It is important to engage in activities that will sustain the shift in culture and help to extend and grow the activities associated with an action research community.
- Examples of these types of activities include grant funding, mini-grants, other incentives, mechanisms for personal and professional growth, and action research conferences.

Where do we go from here? **101**

- Grants can be used to support the work of an action research learning community.
- Action research can be incorporated into a grant proposal as the mechanism for investigating the effectiveness of innovative practices.
- Mini-grants can be used to support the action research efforts of educators in a school or district.
- Mini-grants could be funded by local businesses and organizations, or as part of a larger, formal grant proposal.
- Incentivizing the work of an action research learning community is critical to its success.
- Time is a critical incentive to provide for teachers and other educators engaged in action research.
- The *Action Research Mentor Portfolio* can serve as an important incentive and resource.
- Action research can be built into personnel evaluation systems as a means for teachers to guide their own professional development, and to be held accountable for such.
- Since we expect teachers to work collaboratively together, we may want to strongly consider evaluating them in a similar manner.
- An integral part of the reflective process of action research is to share and communicate the results of your studies.
- Communicating the results of action research can be done in small informal settings, such as grade-level meetings and school-wide faculty meetings, or they can be shared in larger formal settings, such as local action research (or innovation) conferences and even state or national conferences.
- It is important to remember that implementation of an ARC represents a cyclical, iterative process; there will be hurdles and challenges along the way, but the potential benefits are immense.

6

USING ARCS TO DEEPEN PROFESSIONAL LEARNING AND IMPROVE STUDENT ACHIEVEMENT

This final, brief section of the book is designed to "tie up some of the loose ends" that you may have when considering the design and implementation of an action research learning community. For example, you might be saying to yourself, "Action research communities sound great and there are some potential benefits, but why would I really want to participate in an ARC or start one in my school?" I believe that there are two straightforward answers to this question. The first deals with action research communities as a means for professional learning. The second addresses how action research communities can result in improved student achievement.

Action research communities as mechanisms for professional learning

Quite frankly, action research represents the epitome of customizable and meaningful professional development. Long gone should be the days of one-size-fits-all professional development for educators. This type of professional development for educators tends to focus more on "training" and less on "learning." The basic logic behind this approach is that everyone and anyone can benefit—*somehow*—from professional development on the same topic. I do not believe that this is the case. For example, imagine for a moment a fictitious school district that announces that a yearlong professional development program for teachers throughout the district will focus on the integration of technology, specifically the use of wikis and blogs, into

104 Using ARCs to deepen professional learning

classroom practice. Consider the situation of a teacher who has maintained her own classroom blog for years, and who is highly effective at doing so. Or, how about the teacher who teaches in a content area for which it is not as feasible or practical to integrate wikis on a daily basis. What do those teachers stand to gain from this year-long professional development program? As a long-time educator, I have often found myself wondering if or to what degree those countless hours of in-service workshops and trainings have ever truly had a positive impact on how or what I teach, or more importantly, how well my students have mastered the content and skills I was teaching (Mertler, 2013b).

We have begun to see a great deal of options available to educators when it comes to professional development. Online professional development modules or entire courses can be purchased—in an "on-demand" format—to serve the needs of individual teachers. However, at the same time, I would argue that while these *may* meet the needs—on the surface—of individual teachers, they are not 'individualized' to the *specific* needs of *that* particular teacher in *that* particular setting or classroom. For example, a professional development module on differentiated instruction may be an appropriate topic for a particular teacher, but still does not factor in the specifics of the differentiated needs of her specific classroom (nor should it be expected to do so). So, the question remains as to how educators can pursue professional growth and development that truly targets their individual wants and needs.

In today's schools, we must operate under the assumption that our professional educators already possess a good deal of professional knowledge and are capable of extending their own learning. Furthermore, there are types of professional learning that capitalize on the mechanism to support educators in terms of what they already know, but also encourage them to develop new knowledge, sometimes on their own. Action research lends itself very nicely to this concept, in that the process requires educators to reflect on and evaluate what they are already doing, to assess their own effectiveness, and then attempt new or different methods to enhance their effectiveness and their students' learning.

The true benefit of action research as professional learning is that it provides the mechanism for an educator to focus his or her professional growth *specifically* on aspects of the teaching–learning process that have been identified by *that* teacher as an immediate need. The focus of not only the action research, but also the professional learning, is on *your* school, *your* classroom, *your* students, and *their* improved achievement. It is *customizable professional development*, designed to meet your specific needs (Mertler, 2013b). Since it is geared specifically toward your needs and the needs of your students, there is the ability to take action *immediately*. Not only is this customizable professional development, but it is also *meaningful* professional development.

If we now throw into the mix the concept of a professional learning community, in my opinion, we have just added the two final necessary ingredients to a highly beneficial system of professional learning—collaboration and support. Assuming the responsibility for one's own professional learning, by identifying and targeting that which is most crucial in a school or classroom, requires collegial support, and perhaps a sense of collaborative work. After all, if you are experiencing a particular struggle in your classroom, I seriously doubt that you are the only teacher on the face of the earth—let alone your own school or district—who has that problem. Collaboration is an incredibly powerful means of identifying, targeting, and resolving those struggles and challenges that we face in our classrooms on a daily basis.

Action research communities are the facilitating mechanism that can pull all of these things together in one unifying initiative.

Action research communities as mechanisms for improving student achievement

It should follow logically from the previous section that, if we are targeting and improving specific aspects of our instruction based on data that we collect from our students, by improving our teaching, we should also be enhancing the learning experiences for students. After all, this was the initial basis for us to determine specifically which aspects of our teaching we wanted to target for improvement. If our students aren't performing well in some aspect of our coursework or class, we want to see that improve.

For example, let us assume that I am a high school biology teacher—which I actually was . . . many, many years ago. Although I loved to teach the processes of mitosis and meiosis, my students always struggled with them. Year in and year out, it did not matter what the particular mix of students was that I had in my class, they did not do well on the unit test that covered these concepts. If we had an action research community in my school, I could have used that structure—along with my colleagues in the science department—to critically evaluate and investigate ways in which I could teach that material differently, reinforce those skills in alternative ways, and possibly come up with a variety of assessments in order to give students alternative mechanisms for demonstrating their mastery. We comprised a relatively small department in my school, and when I think back to the potential growth and learning—from both the teachers *and* the students—that we might have experienced had we been part of an action research community, my mind races with possibilities.

Because action research can be individualized and it is so customizable, action research learning communities provide an incredible opportunity for schools to target a wide variety of reform initiatives and innovations. Whereas some schools might focus their professional learning communities on very specific curricular and/or social initiatives, schools that operate using an action research learning community have the ability not only to target a variety of initiatives, but those initiatives can develop, change, and transform over time. However, the important feature here is that the basic structure of the action research community does not have to change year in and year out. In fact, the infrastructure of an action research community can remain intact, theoretically for decades. The reason for this is that the fundamental structure of an action research community—action research and collaboration within the environment of a professional learning community—becomes the mechanism for achieving an immense variety of school reform initiatives.

The power and potential that lies within your school and its staff once you undertake the development and implementation of an action research learning community is simply limitless.

Important takeaways from Chapter 6

- Action research represents the epitome of customizable and meaningful professional development.

Using ARCs to deepen professional learning **107**

- Action research can serve as the mechanism for teachers to individualize their own professional learning, in order to focus on their specific needs.
- Action research as professional learning is geared specifically toward your needs and the needs of your students; action can be taken immediately.
- Action research communities take these beneficial concepts of customizable and meaningful professional development and add collegial support and collaboration, forming an extremely powerful learning community structure.
- Action research communities are the facilitating mechanism that can pull all of these components together in one unifying initiative.
- It follows logically that if action research communities improve teaching, the structure can also support and lead to improved academic achievement.
- An action research learning community serves as an overarching structure for a wide variety of reform initiatives and innovations.
- These reform initiatives and innovations may change over time, but the action research community can remain as the foundational structure for professional learning and collaboration in a school.
- Action research and collaboration within an environment of a professional learning community can be a driving mechanism for achieving a wide variety of school reform initiatives.
- The potential that lies within your school once an action research learning community has begun is limitless.

REFERENCES

City, E. A. (2010). Will unbundling provide the best education for all? *Kappan*, *92*(3), 62–64.

City, E. A., Elmore, R. F., Fiarman, S. E., & Teitel, L. (2009). *Instructional rounds in education: A network approach to improving teaching and learning.* Cambridge, MA: Harvard Education Press.

Clauset, K. H., Lick, D. W., & Murphy, C. U. (2008). *Schoolwide action research for professional learning communities: Improving student learning through the whole-faculty study groups approach.* Thousand Oaks, CA: Corwin.

Creswell, J. W. (2005). *Educational research: Planning, conducting, and evaluating quantitative and qualitative research* (2nd ed.). Upper Saddle River, NJ: Merrill/Prentice Hall.

Creswell, J. W., & Plano Clark, V. L. (2011). *Designing and conducting mixed methods research* (2nd ed.). Los Angeles: Sage.

DuFour, R., DuFour, R., & Eaker, R. (2008). *Revisiting professional learning communities at work: New insights for improving schools.* Bloomington, IN: Solution Tree.

DuFour, R., DuFour, R., Eaker, R., & Many, T. (2006). *Learning by doing: A handbook for professional learning communities at work.* Bloomington, IN: Solution Tree.

DuFour, R., & Eaker, R. (1998). *Professional learning communities at work: Best practices for enhancing student achievement.* Bloomington, IN: Solution Tree.

Gay, L. R., Mills, G. E., & Airasian, P. (2009). *Educational research: Competencies for analysis and applications* (9th ed.). Upper Saddle River, NJ: Merrill.

Godin, S. (2011). *Poke the box.* Do You Zoon, Inc.

Henriksen, D., & Richardson, C. (2016). *Design thinking and the practicing teacher: Addressing educational problems of practice.* Manuscript submitted for publication.

Johnson, A. P. (2012). *A short guide to action research* (4th ed.). Boston: Pearson.

Lampert, M. (1985). How do teachers manage to teach?: Perspectives on problems in practice. *Harvard Educational Review*, *55*(2), 178-194.

Lee, K. J. (2013). Action research project resources. *The Finnish Choice of Vocational Schools.* Retrieved January 30, 2014, from www.fulbrightin finland.com/action-research-project-resources.html.

110 References

McMillan, J. H. (2012). *Educational research: Fundamentals for the consumer* (6th ed.). Boston: Allyn & Bacon.

McNiff, J. (2002). *Action research for professional development: Concise advice for new action researchers* (3rd ed.). Dorset, England: Author. Retrieved May 18, 2016, from www.jeanmcniff.com/userfiles/file/Publications/AR%20Booklet.doc

Mertler, C. A. (2005). The role of classroom experience in preservice and inservice teachers' assessment literacy. *Mid-Western Educational Researcher, 18*(4), 25–34.

Mertler, C. A. (2007). *Interpreting standardized test scores: Strategies for data-driven instructional decision making.* Thousand Oaks, CA: Sage.

Mertler, C. A. (2009a). A systematic approach to transforming the art of teaching into the science of teaching: Developing a D-DIDM mindset (MWERA 2008 Presidential Address). *Mid-Western Educational Researcher, 22*(1), 12, 17–23.

Mertler, C. A. (2009b). Teachers' assessment knowledge and their perceptions of the impact of classroom assessment professional development. *Improving Schools, 12*(2), 101–113.

Mertler, C. A. (2010). Teachers' perceptions of the influence of No Child Left Behind on classroom practices. *Current Issues in Education, 13*(3). Available online: http://cie.asu.edu/ojs/index.php/cieatasu/article/viewFile/392/31

Mertler, C. A. (2011, February). *Transformational innovation in education: Empowerment as a first step.* 2011 Keynote Address, Eastern Educational Research Association, Sarasota, Florida.

Mertler, C. A. (2013a). *Action research and educator empowerment: A blueprint for transforming your practice* [iPad 4 version]. Available in the iBookstore. Retrieved from https://itunes.apple.com/us/book/action-research-educator-empowerment/id610086739?ls=1

Mertler, C. A. (2013b). Classroom-based action research: Revisiting the process as customizable and meaningful professional development for educators. *Journal of Pedagogic Development, 3*(3), 39–43. Available online: www.beds.ac.uk/

Mertler, C. A. (2015). *Action research mentor portfolio.* Available in the Teachers Pay Teacher Store. Retrieved from www.teacherspayteachers.com/Product/Action-Research-Mentor-Portfolio-2285854

Mertler, C. A. (2016). *Introduction to educational research.* Los Angeles: Sage.

Mertler, C. A., & Hartley, A. J. (2017). Classroom-based, teacher-led action research as a process for enhancing teaching and learning. Journal of Educational Leadership in Action, 4(2). Available online: www.lindenwood.edu/academics/beyond-the-classroom/publications/journal-of-educational-leadership-in-action

Mertler, C. A. (2017). *Action research: Improving schools and empowering educators* (5th ed.). Los Angeles: Sage.

Mills, G. E. (2014). *Action research: A guide for the teacher researcher* (5th ed.). Boston: Pearson.

Oliver, B. (1980). Action research for inservice training. *Educational Leadership, 37*(5), 394–395.

Parsons, R. D., & Brown, K. S. (2002). *Teacher as reflective practitioner and action researcher.* Belmont, CA: Wadsworth/Thomson Learning.

Robinson, K. (2006, June). *How schools kill creativity* (TED Talks). Available at: http://new.ted.com/talks/ken_robinson_says_schools_kill_creativity

APPENDIX

Action research mentor portfolio templates

As mentioned in Chapter 5, this Appendix consists of seven templates, designed to help educators through various components of the action research process. The templates provide guiding questions or prompts that facilitate various aspects of—and decisions that must be made within—these processes. These templates are also available in electronic, PDF format on the website TeachersPayTeachers.com (www. teacherspayteachers.com/Product/Action-Research-Mentor-Portfolio-2285854)—providing templates to guide teachers through a more formal process of classroom-based action research—is presented and summarized at Chapter 5.

The *Action Research Mentor Portfolio* provides guidance in making these decisions throughout various stages of conducting action research. Focused questions and prompts guide the user through this decision-making process. There are four stages of the action research process: the planning stage, the acting stage, the developing stage, and reflecting stage. Important decisions must be made during each of these four stages. Organized by these four stages, specific aspects of the action research process where the user can obtain direction and mentorship include:

The Planning Stage

- The 5 Why Process for Problem Identification
- Organizing Your Literature Review
- Developing a Research Plan

114 Appendix

The Acting Stage

- Planning for Data Collection
- Planning for Data Analysis

The Developing Stage

- Action Planning

The Reflecting Stage
- Reflecting on the Action Research Process

Once the user has answered the questions and addressed each prompt, "pages" can be printed or emailed (for example, to a professor, advisor, supervisor, or administrator).

The Introduction to the *Action Research Mentor Portfolio* is presented on the next page, followed by each of the seven developmental templates.

Classroom- and school-based action research

Overview of action research in schools

Action research is defined as systematic inquiry conducted by educators at any level (e.g., PK-12, higher education) and in any position (e.g., teachers, administrators, counselors, resource teachers, lead teachers, etc.) who have a vested interest in the success and improvement of any and all aspects of the teaching learning cycle. Action research is a cyclical process of **systematic and scientific inquiry** into professional practice. It consists of four stages—the planning stage, the acting stage, the developing stage, and the reflecting stage. It is an important endeavor for educators at all levels for so many reasons. It can bridge the gap between theory and practice; it has the potential to result in the direct improvement of educational practice; it has a direct connection to school improvement; it helps to empower educators and to stimulate intellectual engagement; and, it is an incredibly important means of experiencing professional growth. Ultimately, it is characterized as research that is conducted **by educators for themselves**. It may truly be the epitome of customizable and meaningful professional development for educators.

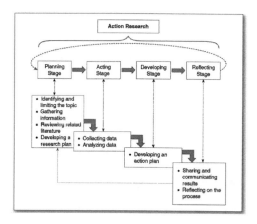

Mertler, C. A. (2017). *Action research: Improving schools and empowering educators* (5th ed.). Los Angeles, CA: Sage.

[PRINT FORM]

© 2015 by Craig A. Mertler, Ph.D.

116 Appendix

Classroom- and school-based action research

"5 why process" for problem identification

Describe a specific problem you have observed in your classroom or school:

Why does/doesn't *this* happen?

Why does/doesn't *this* happen?

Why does/doesn't *this* happen?

Why does/doesn't *this* happen?

Why does/doesn't *this* happen?

Stop the "5 Why Process" when you believe you have identified the root cause of the original problem.

PRINT FORM

SAVE FORM

© 2015 by Craig A. Mertler, Ph.D.

Appendix **117**

Classroom- and school-based action research

Examining background information & related literature

Introduction:

Describe your overall topic, why it is important, and why *you* are interested in it:

List any major themes, subtopics, or trends research questions, methodologies, results and/or conclusions:

Body:

Theme #1:

Characteristics of this theme:

Supporting literature:

118 Appendix

Theme #2:

Characteristics of this theme:

Supporting literature:

Theme #3:

Characteristics of this theme:

Supporting literature:

Theme #4:

Characteristics of this theme:

Supporting literature:

Appendix 119

Theme #5:
Characteristics of this theme:
Supporting literature:

Other supporting background information (from personal experiences, etc.):
Characteristics of this theme:
Supporting evidence:

PRINT FORM

SAVE FORM

© 2015 by Craig A. Mertler, Ph.D.

Classroom- and school-based action research

Developing a research plan

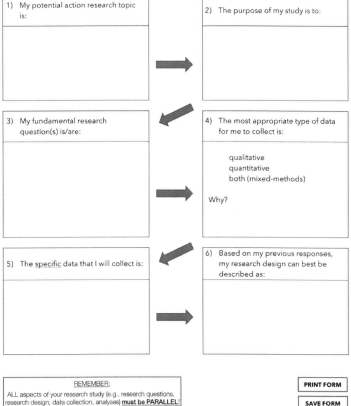

1) My potential action research topic is:

2) The purpose of my study is to:

3) My fundamental research question(s) is/are:

4) The most appropriate type of data for me to collect is:

   qualitative
   quantitative
   both (mixed-methods)

   Why?

5) The specific data that I will collect is:

6) Based on my previous responses, my research design can best be described as:

REMEMBER:
ALL aspects of your research study (e.g., research questions, research design, data collection, analyses) **must be PARALLEL!**

PRINT FORM

SAVE FORM

© 2015 by Craig A. Mertler, Ph.D.

Appendix **121**

Classroom- and school-based action research

Planning for data collection

1) My action research topic is:	2) My research question(s) is/are:

3) Important demographic variables (if any) include:	4) The instrumentation needed to answer my research question(s) can best be described as:

5) The following <u>must</u> be considered in my data collection process in order to answer my question(s):	6) Other potential data collections concerns I have include:

REMEMBER:
ALL aspects of your research study (e.g., research questions, research design, data collection, analyses) **must be PARALLEL!**

PRINT FORM

SAVE FORM

© 2015 by Craig A. Mertler, Ph.D.

Classroom- and school-based action research

Planning for data analysis

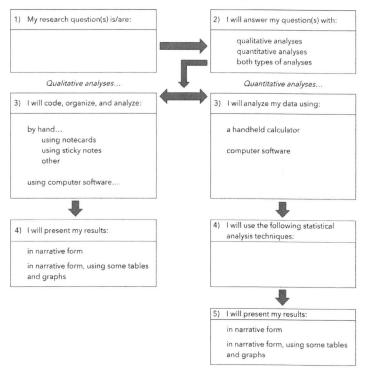

© 2015 by Craig A. Mertler, Ph.D.

Classroom- and school-based action research

Action planning

1) The purpose of my study was to:	2) My research question(s) was/were:

3) A summary of my research findings include:	4) Something I learned from my study was:

5) Recommendations for changes to my practice include:	6) Recommendations for future cycles of action research include:

REMEMBER:
ALL aspects of your research study (e.g., research questions, research design, data collection, analyses) **must be PARALLEL!**

PRINT FORM

SAVE FORM

© 2015 by Craig A. Mertler, Ph.D.

124 Appendix

Classroom- and school-based action research

Professional reflection

1) The purpose of my study was to…	2) I learned the following about my initial problem…
3) Things I learned about my professional practice are…	4) Things I learned about action research are…
5) Things I learned about myself include…	6) When I conduct action research again, I will…

REMEMBER:
ALL aspects of your research study (e.g., research questions, research design, data collection, analyses) **must be PARALLEL**!

PRINT FORM

SAVE FORM

© 2015 by Craig A. Mertler, Ph.D.

INDEX

action research: action plan, developing 28; concept of 1; cyclical process of 22, 23; data, analyzing 27–28; definition 13–14; description of 5–6; developing a research plan 26–27; *vs.* educational research 7–13; gathering information 26; identifying and limiting the topic 25–26; plan and collecting data, implementing 27; process of 21–29; professional benefits of 14–21; reflecting on process 28–29; reviewing the related literature 26; sharing and communicating the results 28; transformational innovation 51–54, 64

action research communities (ARCs) 2; action research/innovation conferences 97–99; align actions with words 81–82; celebrations 85–86; coalition 82–83; conceptual diagram of 67–69; existing practices 80; grant funding 89–90; implementation of 99–100; improving student achievement 105–106; integrating technology 87–88; learning 84–85; mini-grants to 90–91; mistakes 83–84; personnel evaluation systems 95–96; for professional learning 103–105; purposes and functioning of 68–70; roles of: building administrators in 74–75; district administrators 75–77;

teachers 71–74; short-term victories 85–86; student engagement 88–89; systems of incentives 91–95; ways to extend 86–99; ways to sustain 79–80

action research learning communities 2

analysis of variance (ANOVA) 9

ARCs *see* action research communities (ARCs)

CAR *see* collaborative action research (CAR)

case studies 10

causal-comparative studies 8

City, E. A. 62

collaborative action research (CAR) 18, 60

collective inquiry 36–37

comparative studies 8

connect theory to practice 17–18

correlational studies 8

courageous professional educators 71

creativity 52

Creswell, J. W. 10

cultivate professional growth 19–21

cultural shifts 42–44

data-driven educational decision-making (D-DEDM) 55–57

dependent variable 8

descriptive statistics 9

descriptive studies 8

DuFour, R. 31, 33, 34, 36, 38, 39, 40, 41, 45, 47, 76, 81

126 Index

Eaker, R. 31, 33, 70
educational improvement 52
educator empowerment 19
empower educators and engage them intellectually 18–19
epitome 21
ethnographic studies 10
experimental research 8

foster broad school improvement 18

Godin, S. 63
grounded theory research studies 10

Henriksen, D. 11
hypotheses 7

improve educational practice 18
independent variable 8
individual educators 20
inferential statistics 9
innovation 53
intellectual engagement 19

Johnson, A. P. 6, 24

Lee, K. 16
logico-inductive analysis 10

Mills, G. E. 6
mixed-methods research 7, 10

nonexperimental research 8

Oliver, B. 20

personnel evaluation systems 95–96
phenomenological studies 10
polyangulation 10
problems 11–12
problems of practice 11–12
professional learning 103–105
professional learning community (PLCs): action orientation 37–38; ARC, 67–68; changing culture 40–45; characteristics of 34–40; collaborative culture 36; collective inquiry 36–37; commitment to continuous improvement 38–39; concept of 1; cultural shifts 42–44; definition 31–34; goals 35–36; mission 35–36; orientation focused on results 39–40; teaching and assessing in 45–49; values 35–36; vision 35–36
professional reflection 61–62
purposeful improvement 40

qualitative approaches 7, 10
quantitative approaches 7, 10

reculturing 41
reflective practice 71
reform 52
regression 9
research-based solutions 72
research design 8
research questions 7
Richardson, C. 11
Robinson, K. 63, 83

scientific method 6
statistical significance 9

think differently 58–59
traditional educational research 6
transformation 52
transformational innovation: action research 51–54; collaboration 59–60; data 57–58; data-driven educational decision-making 55–57; professional reflection 61–62; subcomponent 62–64; think differently 58–59
triangulation 9
true profession 71
t-tests 9

ultra-creative brainstorming 58

variables 7